W9-BEN-782

Table of Contents

Table of Contents

Name: _____

Vocabulary Building: Prefixes

A **prefix** is a syllable at the beginning of a word that changes its meaning.

Directions: Add the prefixes to the root words to make new words. The first one has been done for you.

PREFIX	MEANING	ROOT WORD	NEW WORD
pre	(before)	caution	precaution
		historic	_____
mid	(middle)	night	_____
		stream	_____
post	(after)	graduate	_____
		war	_____

Directions: Using the meanings in parentheses, complete each sentence with one of the words you formed above. The first one has been done for you.

1. The dog howled at the moon at _____midnight_____ . (middle of the night, 12 o'clock)

2. You must take every _____ when working with chemicals. (care taken in advance)

3. She plans to do _____ work in medicine. (a course of study after graduation)

4. The dinosaur was the biggest _____ animal. (the time before recorded history)

5. While wading, he lost his shoe _____ . (in the middle of a stream)

6. The country made great progress during the early _____ years. (after a war)

Name: _____

Vocabulary Building: Prefixes

Directions: Read the meanings of the following prefixes. Use each word in the box to complete the sentences. Then write another sentence using the word.

PREFIX	re	un	dis
MEANING	(again)	(not)	(apart, away)

regain	retract	undesirable	disclose
undisciplined	discontinue	unexpected	disillusion

1. She was able to _____ her composure after the accident.

   _____

2. I'm afraid we'll have to _____ that line of products due to low sales.

   _____

3. She was surprised by her cousin's _____ visit.

   _____

4. He was bound by law to never _____ top secret information.

   _____

5. The _____ children ran around the grocery store knocking cans off the shelves.

   _____

6. The newspaper decided to _____ the damaging statements printed about the senator.

   _____

7. Those apples look completely _____ with all those bruises.

   _____

8. "I don't want to _____ you," he told her, "but the job isn't quite what you thought it would be."

   _____

Vocabulary Building: Prefixes

Directions: Read the meanings of the following prefixes. Add a prefix to each word in the box to make a new word that makes sense in each sentence. Use the meanings in parentheses to help.

PREFIX	MEANING
extra	beyond
inter	between
sub	below
super	above, outside
trans	across, over

marine	plant	ordinary	natural	zero	national

1. We're planning to _____ the lilac bush from our front yard into our back yard. (move from one place and plant in another)

2. The book was translated and became an _____ bestseller. (between or among nations)

3. Few animals can survive the _____ temperatures in Antarctica. (below zero)

4. The _____ dove deep to avoid enemy fire. (sailing vessel that can operate beneath the water)

5. He made an _____ effort to win the race. (beyond the ordinary)

6. The empty chair moved, apparently guided by some _____ force. (occurring outside the known forces of nature)

Vocabulary Building: Combining Forms

A **combining form** is a word or word base used in forming words, such as **tele** in **telephone**.

Directions: Read the meanings of the combining forms. After each sentence, write the meaning for the bold word. Use a dictionary if needed. The first one has been done for you.

FORM	MEANING
uni	one, single
bi	two
tri	three
quad	four
octo	eight
dec	ten
centi	hundred

1. Do you believe the **unicorn** ever truly existed?

   <u>a mythical animal with one horn</u>

2. It took a **decade** for the oak tree to grow as tall as our house.

   _____

3. On our math test, we had to find the area of a **quadrangle**.

   _____

4. The **centipede** scurried under the refrigerator when the kitchen light was turned on.

   _____

5. The three streets come together to form a **triangle** around our farm.

   _____

6. An **octopus** is a most unusual looking animal!

   _____

Name: _____

Vocabulary Building: Combining Forms

Directions: Circle the combining form in each word, then use the word in a sentence.

FORM	MEANING
auto	self or self-propelled
micro	very small
petr or petro	rock or stone
tele	operating at a distance

Automatic: _____

Automobile: _____

Automotive: _____

Microphone: _____

Microscope: _____

Petrify: _____

Petroleum: _____

Telegram: _____

Telescope: _____

Television: _____

Name: _____

Vocabulary Building: Suffixes "ance" and "ous"

A **suffix** is a syllable at the end of a word that changes its meaning. Suffixes are often used to change a word to a different part of speech, such as from a verb to a noun or a noun to an adjective. The suffix **ance** means "the condition or state of being"; **ous** means "characterized by."

Directions: Add one of the suffixes to the word in parentheses to form a new word that makes sense in the sentence. The first one has been done for you.

1. Mary was very (nerve) _____nervous_____ the night before she starred in the class play.

2. The foolish young man spent all of his (inherit) _____ on a car.

3. The girl's (resemble) _____ to her mother is amazing.

4. A (mystery) _____ woman in black entered the room but said nothing.

5. Tonight is the final (perform) _____ of the opera.

6. Jimmy told the most (outrage) _____ story about why he didn't have his homework.

7. The Grand Canyon is a (marvel) _____ sight.

8. The marriage of Joyce and Ted was a (joy) _____ occasion.

9. I am going to use my (allow) _____ to buy a Mother's Day gift.

10. The American colonists were very (courage) _____ people.

Vocabulary Building: Suffixes "an," "ian," "ship"

The suffixes **an** and **ian** mean "belonging to or living in," and the suffix **ship** means "the quality of or having the office of."

Directions: Combine the suffix and the root word to form a new word.

ROOT WORD	SUFFIX	NEW WORD	ROOT WORD	SUFFIX	NEW WORD
magic	ian	_____	music	ian	_____
America	an	_____	Europe	an	_____
friend	ship	_____	leader	ship	_____

Directions: Use the words you formed to complete the sentences. Then write another sentence using the word.

1. Many _____ settlers came to America to escape persecution in their home countries.

   _____

2. The _____ drew gasps from the audience as he began to saw the woman in half.

   _____

3. Dr. Mathews hopes that his new position on the school board will help him to assume a _____ role in the community.

   _____

4. Over the many years they knew each other, their _____ remained strong.

   _____

5. After years of practicing the piano daily, she has become a fine _____ .

   _____

6. All _____ citizens should exercise their right to vote.

   _____

Vocabulary Building: "ment," "tion," "ence"

Directions: Add the suffixes **ment**, **tion** or **ence** to the words in the box. Then complete the sentences using the new words.

govern	connect	locate	excite
entertain	exist	correspond	concoct

1. The yearly fair created much _____ in the small town.

2. She could not even imagine the _____ being created in the kitchen.

3. Someday, she decided, she would get into politics and work for
   the _____ .

4. The _____ for the evening included dancing, singing and a
   swing band.

5. I had fallen so far behind in my _____ , I hadn't written a letter for
   months.

6. It seemed like a lonely _____ , but she insisted she loved living alone
   in the mountains.

7. The telephone _____ was severed as the construction people worked
   on the road.

8. That is the perfect _____ for that restaurant, for there is no other Italian
   food within miles.

Name: _____

Vocabulary Building: Suffixes "ism" and "ist"

The suffix **ism** means "the condition of being" or "having the characteristics of." The suffix **ist** means "one who does or is skilled at something."

Directions: Combine the suffix and root word to form a new word. Use the new word in a sentence.

1. national + ism: _____

_____

2. patriot + ism: _____

_____

3. alcohol + ism: _____

_____

4. criticize + ism: _____

_____

5. archaeology + ist: _____

_____

6. violin + ist: _____

_____

7. terror + ist: _____

_____

8. chemistry + ist: _____

_____

9. piano + ist: _____

_____

Name: _____

Review

Directions: Add one of the prefixes, suffixes or combining forms to a word in the box to complete each sentence. Use the definition in parentheses as a clue.

ian   ous   ship   an   ist   extra   trans   pre   micro   super

| friend | music | geology | sensory | America |
| paid | wave | market | atlantic | danger |

1. The _____ has a huge selection of fruits and vegetables. (large food store)

2. The first _____ flight was a remarkable feat in the history of aviation. (across the Atlantic Ocean)

3. The woman claimed that she knew the future because of her _____ capabilities. (beyond the normal senses)

4. When mailing your payment, please use the _____ envelope. (paid in advance)

5. Mrs. Johnson studied the violin for many years to become the accomplished _____ she is today. (person skilled in music)

6. The _____ oven is a modern-day convenience. (operating with extremely small electromagnetic waves)

7. Lightning is the most _____ part of a storm. (characterized by danger)

8. They raised the _____ flag over their campground in a gesture of patriotism. (belonging to America)

9. The Native Americans would often smoke a peace pipe as a sign of _____ . (the state of being friends)

10. Dr. Stokes is the finest _____ at the university. (one who is skilled at geology, the study of the earth's crust)

Review

Directions: Add one of the following prefixes or suffixes to the words in the box to complete each sentence. Use the definition in parentheses as a clue.

| tion | al | ment | ence | re | un | dis |

establish	place	estimate
courage	persist	acceptable

1. He will _____ the broken vase next week. (take the place of)

2. I will not _____ you from traveling to Europe. (not persuade)

3. The restaurant on the corner is the newest eating _____ in the city. (business)

4. Your _____ of the amount of money in the jar is surprisingly accurate. (appraisal)

5. Her poor work is _____ . (not allowable)

6. His _____ paid off when he graduated with his doctoral degree. (steadfast effort)

Directions: Write at least two words for each of the following suffixes, then write a sentence for each.

ism _____

_____

ish _____

_____

Name: _____

Vocabulary Building: Homographs

A **homograph** has the same spelling as another word but a different meaning. The two words are often different parts of speech.

Directions: Write the definition from the box for the bold word in each sentence.

con' tract	n.	an agreement to do something
con tract'	v.	to reduce in size, shrink
des' ert	n.	dry land that can support little plant and animal life
de sert'	v.	to abandon
Po' lish	adj.	of or belonging to Poland
pol' ish	v.	to smooth and brighten by rubbing
proj' ect	n.	a proposal or undertaking
pro ject'	v.	to send forth in thoughts or imagination

1. Iron is one of the metals that **contracts** as it cools.

   _____

2. You will have to sign a **contract** before I can begin work on your house.

   _____

3. The **desert** seems to come to life in the evening when the animals come out in search of food.

   _____

4. I hope you will not **desert** your friends now that they really need your support.

   _____

5. She will **polish** the stone and then use it to make a necklace.

   _____

6. The **Polish** people have been courageous in their struggle for freedom.

   _____

7. **Project** yourself into the world of tomorrow with this amazing invention!

   _____

8. I started this **project** on Monday, but it may be weeks before I finish it.

   _____

Name: _____

Vocabulary Building: Homographs

Directions: After each sentence, write the meaning of the bold word. Write another sentence using a homograph for the word.

1. The owner of the pet store tied a bright red
   bow around the puppies' necks.

Meaning: _____

Sentence: _____

2. Today, fewer pipes are made from **lead**.

Meaning: _____

Sentence: _____

3. Marcia's new house is very **close** to ours.

Meaning: _____

Sentence: _____

4. Please **record** the time and day that we finished the project.

Meaning: _____

Sentence: _____

5. It takes only a **minute** to fasten your seatbelt, but it can save your life.

Meaning: _____

Sentence: _____

6. I cannot **subject** the animal to that kind of treatment.

Meaning: _____

Sentence: _____

Vocabulary Building: Multiple Meanings

Directions: Use a dictionary to choose the correct definition for each bold word. The first one has been done for you.

1. My grandfather always has his **spectacles** perched on his nose.

   Meaning: <u>lenses worn in front of the eyes to aid vision</u>

2. The Fourth of July fireworks display was an amazing **spectacle**.

   Meaning: _____

3. We enjoy a rugged vacation, staying in a hunting **lodge** rather than a hotel.

   Meaning: _____

4. Don't let the baby have hard candy, because it could **lodge** in his throat.

   Meaning: _____

5. Termites will **bore** through the rotten wood in our basement if we don't have it replaced.

   Meaning: _____

6. That television show could **bore** even a small child!

   Meaning: _____

7. Don't **resort** to lies just to get what you want!

   Meaning: _____

8. The **resort** is packed with tourists from May to September each year.

   Meaning: _____

Name: _____

Vocabulary Building: Multiple Meanings

Directions: Read each sentence, then write another sentence using a different meaning for the bold word.

1. The prince will **succeed** his mother as ruler of the country.

   _____

2. All through the National Anthem, Johnny was singing in the wrong **key**.

   _____

3. There has been only a **trace** of rain this month.

   _____

4. I can't get involved in a **cause** in which I don't really believe.

   _____

5. It is very important to get plenty of **iron** in your diet.

   _____

6. A police officer can **issue** a warning to those disturbing the peace.

   _____

7. There is a mayoral candidate from each of the major political **parties**.

   _____

8. You can take that **stack** of newspapers to be recycled.

   _____

9. The judge will likely **sentence** the offender to a year in prison.

   _____

10. The lawyer made a **motion** to have the charges dropped.

    _____

Name: _____

Vocabulary Building: Similes

A **simile** is a figure of speech comparing two things using **like** or **as**.

Example: The child was as quiet as a mouse.

Directions: Read the following paragraph. Underline the similes.

    The kittens were born on a morning as cold as ice. Although it was late spring, the weather hadn't quite warmed up. There were five kittens in the litter, each quite different from its siblings. The oldest was black as deepest night. There was a calico that looked like Grandma's old quilt. One was as orange as a fall pumpkin, and another was orange and white. The runt was a black and gray tiger. She was as little as a baseball and as quick as lightning to fight for food. The kittens will soon become accepted by the other animals as members of the farm.

Directions: Using the following words, create similes of your own.

Example: piano—The piano keys tinkled like a light rain on a tin roof.

1. fire _____

_____

2. thunderstorm _____

_____

3. ocean _____

_____

4. night _____

_____

5. rainforest _____

_____

6. giraffe _____

_____

Vocabulary Building: Metaphors

A **metaphor** is a figure of speech that directly compares one thing with another.

Example: As it set, the sun was a glowing orange ball of fire.

The sun is being compared to a glowing orange ball of fire.

sun   _glowing orange ball of fire_

Directions: Underline the metaphor in each sentence.
Then write the two things that are being compared on the lines.

1. The ocean, a swirling mass of anger, released its fury on the shore.

    _____   _____

2. He was a top spinning out of control.

    _____   _____

3. The heat covered the crowd, a blanket smothering them all.

    _____   _____

4. I fed my dog a steak, and it was a banquet for her senses.

    _____   _____

5. The flowers in the garden were a stained glass window.

    _____   _____

Name: _____

Vocabulary Building: Metaphors and Similes

Directions: Underline the metaphors in the following sentences. Then rewrite each sentence using a simile.

1. She is a playful child, a real kitten!

   _____

2. Life today is a merry-go-round.

   _____

3. His emotions were waves washing over him.

   _____

4. His childhood was an image in a rearview mirror.

   _____

Directions: Write the meanings of the following sentences.

1. His mind was as changeable as spring weather.

   _____

2. His demand was like a clap of thunder.

   _____

3. There was joy written on the children's faces on Christmas morning.

   _____

Reading Skills: Personification

When an author gives an object or animal human characteristics, it is called **personification**.

Example: The dragon quickly <u>thought</u> out its next move in the attack on the village.

Thought is a human process and not associated with mythical creatures, therefore; the dragon is personified in that sentence.

Directions: In the following sentences, underline the personification.

1. The cave's gaping mouth led to internal passageways.

2. The tractor sprang to life with a turn of the key.

3. The lights blinked twice and then died.

4. Crops struggled to survive in the blistering heat, hoping for rainfall.

5. The engine of the car coughed and sputtered as if it wanted to breathe but couldn't.

6. The arrow flew through the air, eyeing its target.

7. Snowmen smile from the safety of their yards.

8. Four-year-old Stephanie's doll sipped tea delicately.

Directions: Write a sentence that personifies the following objects.

1. flower _____

2. stuffed animal _____

3. car _____

Name: _____

Reading Skills: Symbolism

Symbolism is the use of something to stand for (symbolize) something else.

Example:

The elderly woman held the pearl necklace in her wrinkled hand and thought back on her life. Many years had gone by since her husband had given her the necklace, as many years as there were pearls. Some of the pearls, she noticed, were darker than others, just as some years in her life had been darker than other years.

The pearl necklace symbolizes the life of the elderly woman. Each pearl stands for a year

in her life, and the necklace represents the many years that have passed.

_____

Directions: Write what is being symbolized in the paragraph on the lines below.

The refugees boarded the small ship with high hopes. They had to believe that their destiny was to find the New World and seek shelter there. A few dared to dream of the riches to be found. For them, the boat itself looked like a treasure chest waiting to be discovered.

_____

_____

_____

For 12-year-old Sam, the basketball court was the best place to be. In Sam's neighborhood, crime ran rampant, and it was the one safe place for kids like Sam to play. Sam spent most nights at the court, practicing lay-ups, jump shots and three-point shots. Sam worked hard because for him it wasn't just a sport, it was a golden key.

_____

_____

_____

Reading Skills: Idioms

An **idiom** is a phrase that says one thing but actually means something quite different.
Example: Now that's <u>a horse of a different color</u>!

Directions: Write the letter of the correct meaning for the bold words in each sentence. The first one has been done for you.

a. forgive and make up	**f.** pressed tightly together
b. fact kept secret for fear of disgrace	**g.** relatives and ancestors
c. something that dampens excitement	**h.** rudely ignored
d. get acquainted, become less formal	**i.** excessive paperwork
e. treated like royalty	**j.** people were gossiping

_g_ 1. There is a pirate and a president in our **family tree**.

_____ 2. The Johnsons went through a lot of **red tape** to adopt their baby.

_____ 3. Sophia gave me the **cold shoulder** when I tried to talk to her this morning.

_____ 4. The big homework assignment threw a **wet blanket** over my plans for an exciting weekend.

_____ 5. At a party, Judy likes to **break the ice** by having her guests play games.

_____ 6. **Tongues were wagging** when the principal called Chet into his office.

_____ 7. There were five people **sandwiched** into the back seat of the car.

_____ 8. She viewed her poor background as **a skeleton in her closet**.

_____ 9. Let's forget our past mistakes and **bury the hatchet**.

_____ 10. When the mayor came to visit our school, we **rolled out the red carpet**.

Name: _____

Reading Skills: Idioms

Directions: Use the following idioms in a sentence of your own. Then tell what the phrase means in your own words.

1. raining cats and dogs

   a. _____

   b. _____

2. going to the dogs

   a. _____

   b. _____

3. barking up the wrong tree

   a. _____

   b. _____

4. hit the nail on the head

   a. _____

   b. _____

5. went out on a limb

   a. _____

   b. _____

6. all in the same boat

   a. _____

   b. _____

7. keep up with the Joneses

   a. _____

   b. _____

Name: _____

Reading Skills: Denotations and Connotations

Sometimes two words can be similar, yet you would not substitute one for the other because they each suggest different feelings.

Denotation means the literal or dictionary definition of a word.

Connotation is the meaning of a word including all the emotions associated with it.

For example, **job** and **chore** are synonyms, but because of their connotations, anyone would choose to do a job instead of a chore.

Directions: Circle the word in each group with the most positive connotation.

Example:

task	old	retort
(job)	mature	respond
chore	antiquated	react

remainder	haughty	conversational
remnants	cheeky	wordy
residue	proud	talkative

excessively	relaxed	shack
grossly	lazy	hovel
abundantly	inactive	hut

curious	swift	scamp
prying	hasty	rascal
nosy	speedy	hoodlum

Name: _____

Reading Skills: Denotations and Connotations

Directions: Replace the bold word in each sentence with a word that has a more positive connotation.

Example:

shut
He ~~slammed~~ the door when he left.

The dog's energy was **uncontrollable**.

We hoped to settle our **fight** peacefully.

The mother **reprimanded** the children when people began to look at them.

The children **gossiped** at lunchtime.

The girl **scribbled** a hasty note to leave behind.

Our conversation ended **abruptly** when the phone rang.

The principal was a **severe** man.

The boy **snatched** the toy from his baby brother.

The couple **rejected** their offer of help.

Dad reminded me to clean my **disastrous** room.

Name: _____

Reading Skills: Denotations and Connotations

Directions: The words in each group have a similar denotation, but one word has a connotation that suggests a negative feeling or idea. Circle the word with the negative connotation. The first one has been done for you.

1. (stun)
   amaze
   astound

2. embarrassed
   ashamed
   blushing

3. chat
   discuss
   gossip

4. mischievous
   playful
   unruly

5. dirty
   filthy
   soiled

6. small
   puny
   miniature

7. abandon
   leave
   depart

Directions: Write the word with the best connotation to complete each sentence.

1. Because he has had the flu for a few days, Mike's face looks very _____ .
   (ghostly, pale, bloodless)

2. We will have to _____ the amount of food we waste.
   (lower, shrink, reduce)

3. Did you get a good _____ from your former employer?
   (reference, mention, recommendation)

4. There was an _____ of measles at our school.
   (attack, occurrence, outbreak)

Name: _____

Review

Directions: Circle the word or phrase that best defines the bold words in each sentence.

1. What is the **subject** of the report you are writing for class?
   to cause to undergo
   topic
   course of study

2. Will you be going to the same **resort** where you spent your vacation last year?
   turn to for use or help
   to sort again
   place for rest and relaxation

3. They **rolled out the red carpet** for the contest winners.
   unrolled carpeting
   treated like royalty
   showed appreciation for

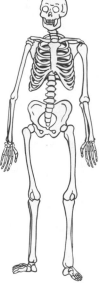

4. Mitch's past as a prisoner was **a skeleton in his closet.**
   fact kept secret for fear of disgrace
   dead person
   ancestor

5. Sally decided to **bury the hatchet** and called her sister to apologize.
   say she was sorry
   forget past mistakes and make up
   go hunting

Directions: Circle the word with the most positive connotation.

6. chat   7. mischievous
   debate   playful
   gossip   unruly

Directions: Underline the simile or metaphor in each sentence. Write **M** for metaphor and **S** for simile.

_____ 8. The clouds looked like cotton candy floating overhead.

_____ 9. Tina was bent out of shape when she was not elected to the school council.

_____ 10. The flute on that album sounds like a rusty gate.

Name: _____

Reading Skills: Classifying

Classifying is placing similar things into categories.

Example: January, May and **October** can be classified as months.

Directions: Write a category name for each group of words.

1. accordion   clarinet   trumpet   _____

2. wasp   bumblebee   mosquito   _____

3. antique   elderly   prehistoric _____

4. chemist   astronomer   geologist   _____

5. nest   cocoon   burrow   _____

Directions: In each row, draw an **X** through the word that does not belong. Then write a sentence telling why it does not belong.

1. encyclopedia   atlas   novel   dictionary

_____

2. bass   otter   tuna   trout

_____

3. sister   grandmother   niece   uncle

_____

4. bark   beech   dogwood   spruce

_____

5. pebble   gravel   boulder   cement

_____

6. spaniel   Siamese   collie   Doberman

_____

Name: _____

Reading Skills: Classifying

Directions: In each row, draw an **X** through the word that does not belong. Then write a word that belongs.

1. monkey   lion   zebra   elephant   grizzly bear   _____

2. daisies   roses   violets   ferns   pansies   _____

3. paper   pear   pencil   eraser   stapler   _____

4. sister   cousin   father   aunt   friend   _____

5. hand   mouth   shirt   foot   elbow   _____

6. shy   cry   happy   angry   sad   _____

7. puppy   dog   kitten   cub   lamb   _____

8. red   blue   color   yellow   purple   _____

9. Earth   Jupiter   Saturn   Pluto   Sun   _____

10. sink   bed   desk   dresser   lamp   _____

Directions: Name each category above.

1. _____   6. _____

2. _____   7. _____

3. _____   8. _____

4. _____   9. _____

5. _____   10. _____

Name: _____

Reading Skills: Classifying

Directions: Write three things that would belong in each category below. The first one has been done for you.

1. mammals

   ___whale___   ___horse___   ___elephant___

2. rainforest animals

   _____   _____   _____

3. capital cities

   _____   _____   _____

4. oceans

   _____   _____   _____

5. occupations

   _____   _____   _____

6. Native American tribes

   _____   _____   _____

7. wars

   _____   _____   _____

8. planets

   _____   _____   _____

9. track and field sports

   _____   _____   _____

10. famous Americans

   _____   _____   _____

Reading Skills: Analogies

An **analogy** is a comparison showing how two things relate to each other. Analogies can show part/whole relationships, antonyms (words with opposite meanings), synonyms (words with the same meaning) and cause/effect relationships. When reading an analogy, say, "Hot is to cold as day is to night." When writing an analogy, use colons.

Example: hot : cold :: day : night

Directions: Complete each analogy using a word from the box.

seize	vault	sleep	cooperative	rich

1. ambush : trap :: catch : _____

2. communicate : tell :: crypt : _____

3. unscrupulous : dishonorable :: docile : _____

4. edible : digestible :: rest : _____

5. mischievous : frolicsome :: wealthy : _____

enhance	private	careless	permit	illogical

6. minority : majority :: public : _____

7. painstaking : haphazard :: selective : _____

8. reduce : increase :: diminish : _____

9. refuse : consent :: deny : _____

10. sane : insane :: logical : _____

Name: _____

Reading Skills: Analogies

Directions: Complete each analogy using a word from the box. The first one has been done for you.

positive	wires	flower	tape	descend	drink	commercial	
grape	house	mouth	rude	bill	melted	worker	four

1. banana : peel :: walnut : _____ shell _____

2. bird : beak :: duck : _____

3. up : ascend :: down : _____

4. cathedral : church :: mansion : _____

5. discourage : encourage :: negative : _____

6. nasal : nose :: oral : _____

7. prune : plum :: raisin : _____

8. hunger : eat :: thirst : _____

9. icicle : frozen :: water : _____

10. dandelion : weed :: lilac : _____

11. polite : impolite :: courteous : _____

12. plumber : pipes :: electrician : _____

13. employer : employee :: boss : _____

14. camera : film :: VCR : _____

15. triangle : three :: square : _____

16. newspaper : advertisement :: television : _____

Name: _____

Reading Skills: Analogies

Directions: Complete each analogy using a word from the box. Write the analogy as a sentence. The first one has been done for you.

engine	herd	frog	soft	White House	wings	boat	garage

1. red : stop :: yellow : _____ caution _____

   Red is to stop as yellow is to caution. _____

2. bird : flock :: cattle : _____

   _____

3. caterpillar : butterfly :: tadpole : _____

   _____

4. queen : palace :: United States president : _____

   _____

5. automobile : wheels :: airplane : _____

   _____

6. astronaut : spacecraft :: sailor : _____

   _____

7. sailboat : wind :: airplane : _____

   _____

8. stone : hard :: grass : _____

   _____

9. airplane : hangar :: automobile : _____

   _____

Reading Skills: Fact or Opinion?

A **fact** is information that can be proved. An **opinion** is information that tells how someone feels or what he/she thinks about something.

Directions: For each sentence, write **F** for fact or **O** for opinion. The first one has been done for you.

_____F_____ 1. Each of the countries in South America has its own capital.

_____ 2. All South Americans are good swimmers.

_____ 3. People like the climate in Peru better than in Brazil.

_____ 4. The continent of South America is almost completely surrounded by water.

_____ 5. The only connection with another continent is a narrow strip of land, called the Isthmus of Panama, which links it to North America.

_____ 6. The Andes Mountains run all the way down the western edge of the continent.

_____ 7. The Andes is the longest continuous mountain barrier in the world.

_____ 8. The Andes are the most beautiful mountain range.

_____ 9. The Amazon River is the second longest river in the world—about 4,000 miles long.

_____ 10. Half of the people in South America are Brazilians.

_____ 11. Life in Brazil is better than life in other South American countries.

_____ 12. Brazil is the best place for South Americans to live.

_____ 13. Cape Horn is at the southern tip of South America.

_____ 14. The largest land animal in South America is the tapir, which reaches a length of 6 to 8 feet.

Name: _____

Reading Skills: Fact or Opinion?

Directions: Read the paragraphs below. For each numbered sentence, write **F** for fact or **O** for opinion. Write the reason for your answer. The first one has been done for you.

(1) The two greatest poems in the history of the world are the *Iliad* and the *Odyssey*. (2) The *Iliad* is the story of the Trojan War; the *Odyssey* tells about the wanderings of the Greek hero Ulysses after the war. (3) These poems are so long that they each fill an entire book.

(4) The author of the poems, according to Greek legend, was a blind poet named Homer. (5) Almost nothing is known about Homer. (6) This indicates to me that it is possible that Homer never existed. (7) Maybe Homer existed but didn't write the *Iliad* and the *Odyssey*.

(8) Whether or not there was a Homer does not really matter. We have these wonderful poems, which are still being read more than 2,500 years after they were written.

1. **O** Reason: This cannot be proven. People have different opinions about which are the greatest poems.

2. _____ Reason: _____

3. _____ Reason: _____

4. _____ Reason: _____

5. _____ Reason: _____

6. _____ Reason: _____

7. _____ Reason: _____

8. _____ Reason: _____

Reading Skills: It's Your Opinion

Your opinion is how you feel or think about something. Although other people may have the same opinion, their reasons could not be exactly the same because of their individuality.

When writing an opinion paragraph, it is important to first state your opinion. Then, in at least three sentences, support your opinion. Finally, end your paragraph by restating your opinion in different words.

Example:

I believe dogs are excellent pets. For thousands of years, dogs have guarded and protected their owners. Dogs are faithful and have been known to save the lives of those they love. Dogs offer unconditional love as well as company for the quiet times in our lives. For these reasons, I feel that dogs make wonderful pets.

Directions: Write an opinion paragraph on whether you would or would not like to have lived in Colonial America. Be sure to support your opinion with at least three reasons.

_____

_____

_____

_____

_____

_____

Writing Checklist

Reread your paragraph carefully.

☐ My paragraph makes sense.   ☐ I have a good opening and ending.

☐ There are no jumps in ideas.   ☐ I used correct spelling.

☐ I used correct punctuation.   ☐ My paragraph is well-organized.

☐ My paragraph is interesting.

Name: _____

Reading Skills: Cause and Effect

A **cause** is the reason something happens. The **effect** is what happens as the result of the cause.

Directions: Read the paragraphs below. For each numbered sentence, circle the cause or causes and underline the effect or effects. The first one has been done for you.

(**1**) All living things in the ocean are endangered by humans polluting the water. Pollution occurs in several ways. One way is the dumping of certain waste materials, such as garbage and sewage, into the ocean. (**2**) The decaying bacteria that feed on the garbage use up much of the oxygen in the surrounding water, so other creatures in the area often don't get enough.

Other substances, such as radioactive waste material, can also cause pollution. These materials are often placed in the water in securely sealed containers. (**3**) But after years of being exposed to the ocean water, the containers may begin to leak.

Oil is another major source of concern. (**4**) Oil is spilled into the ocean when tankers run aground and sink or when oil wells in the ocean cannot be capped. (**5**) The oil covers the gills of fish and causes them to smother. (**6**) Diving birds get the oil on their wings and are unable to fly. (**7**) When they clean themselves, they are often poisoned by the oil.

Rivers also can contribute to the pollution of oceans. Many rivers receive the runoff water from farmlands. (**8**) Fertilizers used on the farms may be carried to the ocean, where they cause a great increase in the amount of certain plants. Too much of some plants can actually be poisonous to fish.

Worse yet are the pesticides carried to the ocean. These chemicals slowly build up in shellfish and other small animals. These animals then pass the pesticides on to the larger animals that feed on them. (**9**) The buildup of these chemicals in the animals can make them ill or cause their babies to be born dead or deformed.

Name: _____

Reading Skills: Cause and Effect

Directions: Read the following cause-and-effect statements. If you think the cause and effect are properly related, write **True**. If not, explain why not. The first one has been done for you.

1. The best way to make it rain is to wash your car.

   It does not rain every time you wash your car.

2. Getting a haircut really improved Randy's grades.

   _____

3. Michael got an "A" in geometry because he spent a lot of time studying.

   _____

4. Yesterday I broke a mirror, and today I slammed my thumb in the door.

   _____

5. Helen isn't allowed to go to the dance tonight because she broke her curfew last weekend.

   _____

6. Emily drank a big glass of orange juice and her headache went away.

   _____

7. The Johnsons had their tree cut down because it had Dutch elm disease.

   _____

8. We can't grow vegetables in our backyard because the rabbits keep eating them.

   _____

Name: _____

Review

Directions: Add another word that belongs in each group.
Then write a category name for each group.

1. soccer   archery   skiing   _____   _____

2. Mercury   Pluto   Venus   _____   _____

3. miniature   shrimpy   dwarfed   _____   _____

4. grasshopper   ant   beetle   _____   _____

5. daisy   chrysanthemum   rose   _____   _____

6. hamburger   chicken   fish   _____   _____

Directions: Complete each analogy.

1. photograph : album :: definition : _____

2. gigantic : big :: tiny : _____

3. fish : school :: geese : _____

4. appetizer : dinner :: preview : _____

5. amplify : intensify :: soften : _____

6. boundless : restricted :: wild : _____

Name: _____

Review

Directions: Write **Fact** or **Opinion** to describe each sentence.

_____ 1. Hurricanes are also known as typhoons.

_____ 2. Hurricanes are the worst natural disasters.

_____ 3. All hurricanes begin over the ocean near the equator.

_____ 4. All people are concerned about pollution.

_____ 5. Pesticides should never be used.

_____ 6. Many colonists died due to lack of food and sickness.

_____ 7. Kites are the best gift to give a child.

_____ 8. The names of Columbus' three ships were the Niña, the Pinta and the Santa Maria.

Directions: If the sentence demonstrates a logical cause and effect relationship, write **Yes** on the line. If the sentence is illogical, write **No**.

_____ 1. I ate fish and got sick, so all fish will make me sick.

_____ 2. The farmer began practicing crop rotation, and his crop yield improved.

_____ 3. I know how to swim, so I cannot possibly drown.

_____ 4. While learning to ski, Jim broke his leg.

_____ 5. The river overflowed its banks and caused much damage.

_____ 6. The Cincinnati Reds won 100 games last year, so they probably will this year.

_____ 7. Because I started using a new toothpaste, I will make more friends.

Writing: Outlining

An **outline** is a skeletal description of the main ideas and important details of a reading selection. Making an outline is a good study aid. It is particularly useful when you must write a paper.

Directions: Read the paragraphs, and then complete the outline below.

Weather has a lot to do with where animals live. Cold-blooded animals have body temperatures that change with the temperature of the environment. Cold-blooded animals include snakes, frogs and lizards. They cannot live anywhere the temperatures stay below freezing for long periods of time. The body temperatures of warm-blooded animals do not depend on the environment. Any animal with hair or fur—including dogs, elephants and whales—are warm-blooded. Warm-blooded animals can live anywhere in the world where there is enough food to sustain them.

Some warm-blooded animals live where snow covers the ground all winter. These animals have different ways to survive the cold weather. Certain animals store up food to last throughout the snowy season. For example, the tree squirrel may gather nuts to hide in his home. Other animals hibernate in the winter. The ground squirrel, for example, stays in its burrow all winter long, living off the fat reserves in its body.

Title: _____

Main Topic: I. _____

   Subtopic: A. Cold-blooded animals' temperatures change with environment.

   Detail: 1. _____

   Subtopic: B. _____

   Detail: 1. They can live anywhere there is food.

Main Topic: II. _____

   Subtopic: A. Animals have different ways to survive the cold.

   Details: 1. _____

         2. _____

Name: _____

Reading Skills: Generalizations

A **generalization** is a statement or rule that applies to many situations or examples.

Example: All children get into trouble at one time or another.

Directions: Read each paragraph, then circle the generalization that best describes the information given.

Although many people think of reptiles as slimy, snakes and other reptiles are covered with scales that are dry to the touch. Scales are outgrowths of the animal's skin. Although in some species they are nearly invisible, in most they form a tile-like covering. The turtle's shell is made up of hardened scales that are fused together. The crocodile has a tough but more flexible covering.

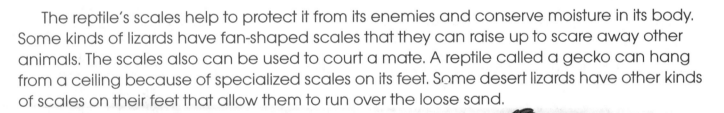

Every reptile has scales.

The scales of all reptiles are alike.

There are many different kinds of scales.

The reptile's scales help to protect it from its enemies and conserve moisture in its body. Some kinds of lizards have fan-shaped scales that they can raise up to scare away other animals. The scales also can be used to court a mate. A reptile called a gecko can hang from a ceiling because of specialized scales on its feet. Some desert lizards have other kinds of scales on their feet that allow them to run over the loose sand.

Scales have many functions.

Scales scare away other animals.

Scales help reptiles adapt to their environments.

A snake will periodically shed its skin, leaving behind a thin impression of its body—scales and all. A lizard sheds its skin too, but it tears off in smaller pieces rather than in one big piece. Before a snake begins this process, which is called molting, its eyes cloud over. The snake will go into hiding until they clear. When it comes out again, it brushes against rough surfaces to pull off the old skin.

Snakes go into hiding before they molt.

Reptiles periodically shed their skin.

A lizard's skin molts in smaller pieces.

Name: _____

Reading Skills: Generalizations

Directions: Identify which statements below are generalizations and which are specific. Write **G** for generalization and **S** for specific.

_____ 1. We want to have lots of good food for the party.

_____ 2. Jenna gave me three pink shirts and two pairs of jeans.

_____ 3. Americans are generous and friendly.

_____ 4. There are ten more female teachers than male teachers at our school.

_____ 5. She wants me to buy watermelon at the grocery store.

_____ 6. She will never believe anything I say.

_____ 7. I got poison ivy because I didn't watch out for the foliage on our hike.

_____ 8. My mom is the best mom in the world.

_____ 9. I get depressed every time the weather turns bad.

_____ 10. The team is so good because they work out and practice every day.

_____ 11. Cats are so bad-tempered.

_____ 12. My dog has a good temperment because he's had lots of training.

_____ 13. Our football team is the best this county has ever seen.

_____ 14. I love the feel of rain on my skin, because it's cool.

_____ 15. That classroom is always out of control.

Name: _____

Writing: Summarizing

A **summary** is a brief retelling of the main ideas of a reading selection. To summarize, write the author's most important points in your own words.

Directions: Write a two-sentence summary for each paragraph.

The boll weevil is a small beetle that is native to Mexico. It feeds inside the seed pods, or bolls, of cotton plants. The boll weevil crossed into Texas in the late 1800s. It has since spread into most of the cotton-growing areas of the United States. The boll weevil causes hundreds of millions of dollars worth of damage to cotton crops each year.

Summary: _____

_____

_____

Each spring, female boll weevils open the buds of young cotton plants with their snouts. They lay eggs inside the buds, and the eggs soon hatch into wormlike grubs. The grubs feed inside the buds, causing the buds to fall from the plant. They eat their way from one bud to another. Several generations of boll weevils may be produced in a single season.

Summary: _____

_____

_____

The coming of the boll weevil to the United States caused tremendous damage to cotton crops. Yet, there were some good results, too. Farmers were forced to plant other crops. In areas where a variety of crops were raised, the land is in better condition than it would have been if only cotton had been grown.

Summary: _____

_____

_____

Writing: Summarizing a Personal Narrative

Directions: Read the following narrative, then follow the directions.

My Greatest Fear

I am scared of spiders. I realize this is not a logical fear, but I cannot help myself. I have been frightened by spiders since I was very young. For the following three reasons, spiders will never be pets of mine. The first reason that I am scared of spiders is their appearance. I do not like their eight wispy, creepy legs. Spiders are never easily seen, but rather dark and unattractive. They are often hairy, and the mere thought of multiple eyeballs gives me shivers.

Spiders are not well-behaved. They are sly and always ready to sneak up on innocent victims. Spiders have habits of scurrying across floors, dropping from ceilings, and dangling from cobwebs. One never knows what to expect from a spider.

Finally, I am scared of spiders due to a "spider experience" as a child. Having just climbed into bed, I noticed a particularly nasty-looking spider on the ceiling over my bed. My father came into dispose of it, and it fell into bed with me. The thought of it crawling over me drove me from the bed shrieking. After that, I checked the ceiling nightly before getting into bed.

Many people love spiders. They are good for the environment and are certainly needed on our planet. However, because of my fear, irrational though it may be, I'd rather just avoid contact with arachnids.

Directions: Write a four-sentence summary of the narrative.

_____

_____

_____

_____

_____

_____

Name: _____

Writing: Summarizing a Personal Narrative

Write the main idea of the second paragraph.

_____

_____

Write the main idea of the third paragraph.

_____

_____

Write the main idea of the fourth paragraph.

_____

_____

Everyone has a fear of something. On another sheet of paper, write a five-paragraph personal narrative about a fear of your own. Use the following guide to help you organize your narrative.

Paragraph 1. State your fear.

Provide background information about fear.

Paragraph 2. State your first reason for fear.

Support this statement with at least three sentences.

Paragraph 3. State your second reason for fear.

Support this statement with at least three sentences.

Paragraph 4. State your third reason for fear.

Support this statement with at least three sentences.

Paragraph 5. Provide a summary of your narrative.

Restate your fear in different words from the opening sentence.

Writing: Paraphrasing

Paraphrasing means to restate something in your own words.

Directions: Write the following sentences in your own words. The first one has been done for you.

1. He sat alone and watched movies throughout the cold, rainy night.

   All through the damp, chilly evening, the boy watched television by himself.

2. Many animals such as elephants, zebras and tigers live in the grasslands.

   _____

   _____

3. In art class, Sarah worked diligently on a clay pitcher, molding and shaping it on the pottery wheel.

   _____

   _____

4. The scientists frantically searched for a cure for the new disease that threatened the entire world population.

   _____

   _____

5. Quietly, the detective crept around the abandoned building, hoping to find the missing man.

   _____

   _____

6. The windmill turned lazily in the afternoon breeze.

   _____

   _____

Name: _____

Writing: Paraphrasing

Directions: Using synonyms and different word order, paraphrase the following paragraphs. The first one has been done for you.

Some of the Earth's resources, such as oil and coal, can be used only once. We should always, therefore, be careful how we use them. Some materials that are made from natural resources, including metal, glass and paper, can be reused. This is called recycling.

Many natural resources, including coal and oil, can be used only one time. For this reason, it is necessary to use them wisely. There are other materials made from resources of the Earth that can be recycled, or used again. Materials that can be recycled include metal, glass and paper.

Recycling helps to conserve the limited resources of our land. For example, there are only small amounts of gold and silver ores in the earth. If we can recycle these metals, less of the ores need to be mined. While there is much more aluminum ore in the earth, recycling is still important. It takes less fuel energy to recycle aluminum than it does to make the metal from ore. Therefore, recycling aluminum helps to conserve fuel.

_____

_____

_____

_____

It is impossible to get minerals and fossil fuels from the earth without causing damage to its surface. In the past, people did not think much about making these kinds of changes to the Earth. They did not think about how these actions might affect the future. As a result, much of the land around mines was left useless and ugly. This is not necessary, because such land can be restored to its former beauty.

_____

_____

_____

_____

Name: _____

Reading Skills: Skimming and Scanning

Skimming is reading quickly to get a general idea of what a reading selection is about. When skimming, look for headings and key words to give you an overall idea of what you are reading.

Scanning is looking for certain words to find facts or answer questions. When scanning, read or think of questions first.

Directions: Scan the paragraphs below to find the answers to the questions. Then look for specific words that will help you locate the answers. For example, in the second question, scan for the word **smallest**.

There are many different units to measure time. Probably the smallest unit that you use is the second, and the longest unit is the year. While 100 years seems like a very long time to us, in the history of the Earth, it is a smaller amount of time than one second is in a person's entire lifetime.

To describe the history of the Earth, scientists use geologic time. Even a million years is a fairly short period in geologic time. Much of the known history of the Earth is described in terms of tens or even hundreds of millions of years. Scientists believe that our planet is about 4,600 million years old. Since a thousand million is a billion, the Earth is said to be 4.6 billion years old.

1. What kind of time is used to describe the history of the Earth?

   _____

2. For the average person, what is the smallest unit of time used?

   _____

3. In millions of years, how old do scientists believe the Earth is?

   _____

4. How would you express that in billions of years?

   _____

Name: _____

Reading Skills: Author's Purpose

An **author's purpose** is the reason why he/she writes a particular story or book. The author usually wants to entertain, inform or persuade the reader. Sometimes the author can have more than one purpose.

Directions: Read each paragraph. Determine the author's purpose for writing it, and write one or more of the following—**inform**, **entertain** or **persuade**.

1. In planning for the wise use of our natural resources, it is helpful for people to know the kind of resource they are using. There are, in general, two groups—renewable and non-renewable resources. Renewable resources, such as plants, can be replaced as they are used. Non-renewable resources include fossil fuels and minerals, which cannot be replaced.

   Purpose: _____

2. It is vitally important that each of us acts now to save our natural resources. The future of our planet depends on it. We must not allow any of these resources to be wasted. Write to your senators today, urging them to pass laws that will ensure that there will be plenty of fuel and clean air and water for future generations.

   Purpose: _____

3. Mother Nature needs you! After millions of years of caring for the needs of humans, Mother Nature now needs our help. She is choking from the polluted air, and her face is scarred and dirtied. So do your part to help your mother—keep the air and waterways clean, and remember to recycle.

   Purpose: _____

Name: _____

Reading Skills: Author's Purpose

Directions: Read the following speeches and write if the speaker is entertaining, informing or persuading his/her audience.

1. Attention fair-goers! For your enjoyment this evening, we have the new band, "Change of Mind," to dazzle you! Straight from Los Angeles, this band has a new sound that will knock you over! Join me in welcoming "Change of Mind"!

   Purpose: _____

2. My friends, the time has come for us to join the fight against this deadly disease. We must commit both ourselves and our dollars to eradicate this disease before it reaches epidemic proportions. Don't procrastinate and find that you regret it later. Please donate to our fund.

   Purpose: _____

3. This year was an excellent one for our company. We created 10 new products and made over $5 billion in profit. We will begin expanding within three months and foresee the creation of 2,000 new jobs.

   Purpose: _____

Write a persuasive paragraph about a rule you believe should be changed. Be sure to provide several supporting sentences.

_____

_____

_____

_____

_____

Name: _____

Using the Right Resources

Directions: Decide where you would look to find information on the following topics. After each question, write one or more of the following references:

- **almanac** — contains tables and charts of statistics and information
- **atlas** — collection of maps
- **card/computer catalog** — library resource showing available books by topic, title or author
- **dictionary** — contains alphabetical listing of words with their meanings, pronunciations and origins
- **encyclopedia** — set of books or CD-ROM with general information on many subjects
- *Readers' Guide to Periodical Literature* — an index of articles in magazines and newspapers
- **thesaurus** — contains synonyms and antonyms of words

1. What is the capital of The Netherlands? _____

2. What form of government is practiced there? _____

3. What languages are spoken there? _____

4. What is the meaning of the word **indigenous**? _____

5. Where would you find information on conservation? _____

_____

6. What is a synonym for **catastrophe**? _____

7. Where would you find a review of the play *Cats*? _____

_____

8. Where would you find statistics on the annual rainfall in the Sahara Desert?

_____

9. What is the origin of the word **plentiful**? _____

10. What are antonyms for the word **plentiful**? _____

11. Where would you find statistics for the number of automobiles manufactured in the United States last year? _____

Review

Directions: Read the paragraph, then follow the directions.

According to one estimate, 75 percent of all fresh water on the Earth is in the form of ice. The polar regions of the Earth are almost completely covered by ice. In some places, the ice is more than 8,000 feet thick. If all of this ice were spread out evenly, the Earth would be covered with a 100-foot-thick layer of ice. Although ice is not an important source of fresh water today, it could be in the future. Some people have proposed towing large, floating masses of ice to cities to help keep up with the demand for fresh water.

1. Complete the outline of the paragraph.

Title: _____

Main Topic: I. 75 percent of fresh water on Earth is ice.

Subtopics: A. _____

B. _____

2. Check the most appropriate generalization:

☐ Ice is the most plentiful source of fresh water.

☐ Ice is important to the future.

3. Paraphrase the first sentence by restating it in your own words.

_____

4. Is the author's purpose to inform, entertain or persuade?

_____

5. Where would you look to find information on the polar ice caps?

_____

Name: _____

Review

Directions: Read the paragraph, then follow the directions.

Constellations are groups of stars that have been given names. They often represent an animal, person or object. One of the easiest constellations to identify is the Big Dipper, which is shaped like a spoon. Once the Big Dipper is located, it is easy to see Cassiopeia (a W), the Little Dipper (an upside-down spoon) and the North Star. The North Star's scientific name is Polaris, and it is the last star in the handle of the Little Dipper. Other constellations include Orion the hunter, Gemini the twins, Canis Major the dog and Pegasus the winged horse. Many ancient cultures, including the Greeks and Native Americans, used the position of the stars to guide them. They also planned daily life activities, such as planting, hunting and harvesting, by the path the constellations made through the sky. For thousands of years, humans have gazed at the sky, fascinated by the millions of stars and imagining pictures in the night.

The Constellation Orion

1. Complete the outline of the paragraph.

Title: _____

Main Topic: I. _____

Subtopics: A. _____

          B. _____

_____

2. In three sentences, summarize the paragraph.

_____

_____

_____

3. What is the author's purpose? _____

4. Under which topics would you look to find more information on constellations?

_____ _____ _____

Name: _____

Review

Directions: Imagine you are making a speech about one of your hobbies. Complete an outline of the speech.

Title: _____

Main Topic: I. _____

Subtopics: A. _____

            B. _____

Who is your audience? _____

Is it appropriately written for that audience? _____

Are you trying to inform, entertain or persuade? _____

In the space below, write your speech in at least 100 words.

_____

_____

_____

_____

_____

_____

_____

_____

Comprehension: Colonists Come to America

After Christopher Columbus discovered America in 1492, many people wanted to come live in the new land. During the 17th and 18th centuries, a great many Europeans, especially the English, left their countries and settled along the Atlantic Coast of North America between Florida and Canada. Some came to make a better life for themselves. Others, particularly the Pilgrims, the Puritans and the Quakers, came for religious freedom.

A group of men who wanted gold and other riches from the new land formed the London Company. They asked the king of England for land in America and for permission to found a colony. They founded Jamestown, the first permanent English settlement in America, in 1607. They purchased ships and supplies, and located people who wanted to settle in America.

The voyage to America took about eight weeks and was very dangerous. Often, fierce winds blew the wooden ships off course. Many were wrecked. The ships were crowded and dirty. Frequently, passengers became ill, and some died. Once in America, the early settlers faced even more hardships.

Directions: Answer these questions about the colonists coming to America.

1. How long did it take colonists to travel from England to America? _____

2. Name three groups that came to America to find religious freedom.

   1) _____ 2) _____ 3) _____

3. Why was the London Company formed? _____

   _____

4. What was Jamestown? _____

   _____

5. Why was the voyage to America dangerous? _____

   _____

Name: _____

Recalling Details: Early Colonial Homes

When the first colonists landed in America, they had to find shelter quickly. Their first homes were crude bark and mud huts, log cabins or dugouts, which were simply caves dug into the hillsides. As soon as possible, the settlers sought to replace these temporary shelters with comfortable houses.

Until the late 17th century, most of the colonial homes were simple in style. Almost all of the New England colonists—those settling in the northern areas of Massachusetts, Connecticut, Rhode Island and New Hampshire—used wood in building their permanent homes. Some of the buildings had thatched roofs. However, they caught fire easily, and so were replaced by wooden shingles. The outside walls also were covered with wooden shingles to make the homes warmer and less drafty.

In the middle colonies—New York, Pennsylvania, New Jersey and Delaware—the Dutch and German colonists often made brick or stone homes that were two-and-a-half or three-and-a-half stories high. Many southern colonists—those living in Virginia, Maryland, North Carolina, South Carolina and Georgia—lived on large farms called plantations. Their homes were usually made of brick.

In the 18th century, some colonists became wealthy enough to replace their simple homes with mansions, often like those being built by the wealthy class in England. They were called Georgian houses because they were popular during the years that Kings George I, George II and George III ruled England. Most were made of brick. They usually featured columns, ornately carved doors and elaborate gardens.

Directions: Answer these questions about early colonial homes.

1. What were the earliest homes of the colonists?

_____

2. What were the advantages of using wooden shingles?

_____

3. What did Dutch and German colonists use to build their homes?

_____

4. What were Georgian homes?

_____

Recalling Details: The Colonial Kitchen

The most important room in the home of a colonial family was the kitchen. Sometimes it was the only room in the home. The most important element of the kitchen was the fireplace. Fire was essential to the colonists, and they were careful to keep one burning at all times. Before the man of the house went to bed, he would make sure that the fire was carefully banked so it would burn all night. In the morning, he would blow the glowing embers into flame again with a bellows. If the fire went out, one of the children would be sent to a neighbor's for hot coals. Because there were no matches, it would sometimes take a half hour to light a new fire, using flint, steel and tinder.

The colonial kitchen, quite naturally, was centered around the fireplace. One or two large iron broilers hung over the hot coals for cooking the family meals. Above the fireplace, a large musket and powder horn were kept for protection in the event of an attack and to hunt deer and other game. Also likely to be found near the fireplace was a butter churn, where cream from the family's cow was beaten until yellow flakes of butter appeared.

The furniture in the kitchen—usually benches, a table and chairs—were made by the man or men in the family. It was very heavy and not very comfortable. The colonial family owned few eating utensils—no forks and only a few spoons, also made by members of the family. The dishes included pewter plates, "trenchers"—wooden bowls with handles—and wooden mugs.

Directions: Answer these questions about the colonial kitchen.

1. What was the most important element of the colonial kitchen? _____

2. In colonial days, why was it important to keep a fire burning in the fireplace?

_____

3. Name two uses of the musket.

    1) _____ 2) _____

4. Who made most of the furniture in the early colonial home?

_____

Sequencing: Spinning

Most of the colonists could not afford to buy clothes sent over from Europe. Instead, the women and girls, particularly in the New England colonies, spent much time spinning thread and weaving cloth to make their own clothing. They raised sheep for wool and grew flax for linen.

In August, the flax was ready to be harvested and made into linen thread. The plants were pulled up and allowed to dry. Then the men pulled the seed pods from the stalks, bundled the stalks and soaked them in a stream for about five days. The flax next had to be taken out, cleaned and dried. To get the linen fibers from the tough bark and heavy wooden core, the stalks had to be pounded and crushed. Finally, the fibers were pulled through the teeth of a brush called a "hatchel" to comb out the short and broken fibers. The long fibers were spun into linen thread on a spinning wheel.

The spinning wheel was low, so a woman sat down to spin. First, she put flax in the hollow end of a slender stick, called the spindle, at one end of the spinning wheel. It was connected by a belt to a big wheel at the other end. The woman turned the wheel by stepping on a pedal. As it turned, the spindle also turned, twisting the flax into thread. The woman constantly dipped her fingers into water to moisten the flax and keep it from breaking. The linen thread came out through a hole in the side of the spindle. It was bleached and put away to be woven into pieces of cloth.

Directions: Number in order the steps to make linen thread from flax.

_____ The woman sat at the spinning wheel and put flax in the spindle.

_____ Seed pods were pulled from the stalks; stalks were bundled and soaked.

_____ In August, the flax was ready to be harvested and made into thread.

_____ The stalks were pounded and crushed to get the linen fibers.

_____ The thread was bleached and put away to be woven into cloth.

_____ The short fibers were separated out with a "hatchel."

_____ The woman dipped her fingers into water to moisten the flax.

_____ The long fibers were spun into linen thread on a spinning wheel.

_____ The woman turned the wheel by stepping on a pedal, twisting the flax into thread.

_____ The plants were pulled up and allowed to dry.

_____ The linen thread came out through a hole in the side of the spindle.

Name: _____

Recalling Details: Clothing in Colonial Times

The clothing of the colonists varied from the north to the south, accounting for the differences not only in climate, but also in the religions and ancestries of the settlers. The clothes seen most often in the early New England colonies where the Puritans settled were very plain and simple. The materials—wool and linen—were warm and sturdy.

The Puritans had strict rules about clothing. There were no bright colors, jewelry, ruffles or lace. A Puritan woman wore a long-sleeved gray dress with a big white color, cuffs, apron and cap. A Puritan man wore long woolen stockings and baggy leather "breeches," which were knee-length trousers. Adults and children dressed in the same style of clothing.

In the middle colonies, the clothing ranged from the simple clothing of the Quakers to the colorful, loose-fitting outfits of the Dutch colonists. Dutch women wore more colorful outfits than Puritan women, with many petticoats and fur trim. The men had silver buckles on their shoes and wore big hats decked with curling feathers.

In the southern colonies, where there were no religious restrictions against fancy clothes, wealthy men wore brightly colored breeches and coats of velvet and satin sent from England. The women's gowns also were made of rich materials and were decorated with ruffles, ribbons and lace. The poorer people wore clothes similar to the simple dress of the New England Puritans.

Directions: Answer these questions about clothing in colonial times.

1. Why did the clothing of the colonists vary from the north to the south?

   _____

2. Why did the Puritans wear very plain clothing?

   _____

3. What was the nationality of many settlers in the middle colonies?

   _____

4. From what country did wealthy southern colonists obtain their clothing?

   _____

Name: _____

Recalling Details: Venn Diagrams

A **Venn diagram** is used to chart information that shows similarities and differences between two things. The outer part of each circle shows the differences. The intersecting part of the circles shows the similarities.

Example:

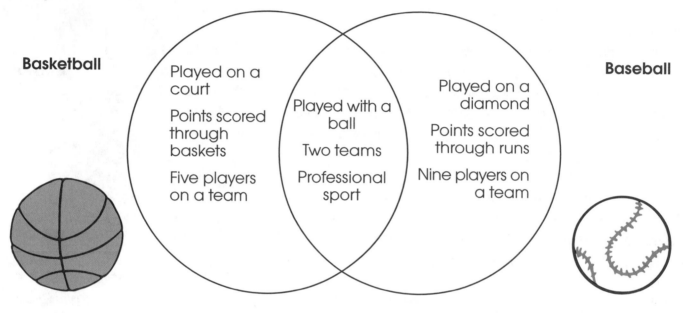

Basketball

Played on a court

Points scored through baskets

Five players on a team

Played with a ball

Two teams

Professional sport

Played on a diamond

Points scored through runs

Nine players on a team

Baseball

Directions: Complete the Venn diagram below. Think of at least three things to write in the outer part of each circle (differences) and at least three things to write in the intersecting part (similarities).

Colonial Kitchen   **Your Kitchen**

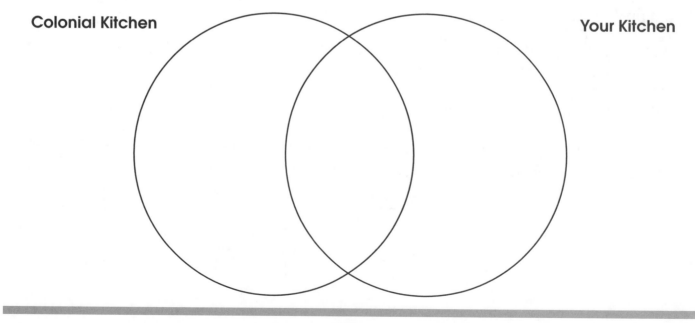

Name: _____

Comprehension: Colonial Schools

In early colonial days, there were no schools or teachers. Children learned what they could at home from their parents, but often their parents couldn't read or write either. Later, some women in the New England colonies began teaching in their homes. These first schools were known as "dame schools." Often the books used in these schools were not books at all, but rather "hornbooks"—flat, paddle-shaped wooden boards with the alphabet or Lord's Prayer on the front.

In 1647, a law was passed in the New England colonies requiring every town of 50 or more families to establish an elementary school. By the 1700s, one-room log schoolhouses were common. Children of all ages studied together under one strict schoolmaster. They attended school six days a week, from 7:00 or 8:00 in the morning until 4:00 or 5:00 in the afternoon. Their only textbooks were the Bible and the *New England Primer*, which contained the alphabet, spelling words, poems and questions about the Bible.

Like the New England colonies, the middle colonies also established schools. However, there were few schools in the southern colonies, where most of the people lived on widely separated farms. Wealthy plantation owners hired private teachers from England to teach their children, but the children of poor families received no education.

Directions: Answer these questions about colonial schools.

1. What was a "hornbook"? _____

_____

2. What was required by the law passed in the New England colonies in 1647?

_____

_____

3. During the 1700s, what textbooks were used in the New England schools?

_____

4. Why was it hard to establish schools in the southern colonies?

_____

Name: _____

Compare/Contrast: Schools

Directions: Think about the differences and similarities between colonial and modern schools. Use the chart below to help organize your ideas. Then, write a paragraph discussing the similarities and a paragraph discussing the differences. The topic sentences have been written for you.

Similarities	Differences

There are several similarities between colonial schools and schools today.

_____

_____

_____

_____

_____

Although there are similarities between colonial schools and modern schools, there are also many differences.

_____

_____

_____

_____

_____

Name: _____

Comprehension: Religion in New England

Many New England colonists had come to America for religious freedom. Religion was very important to them. One of the first buildings erected in any new settlement was a church, or meetinghouse. They were generally in the center of town and were used for public meetings of all kinds. These early meetinghouses were plain, unpainted wood buildings. Later churches were larger and more elaborate. They were usually painted white and had tall, graceful bell towers rising from the roof.

Although they came to America to have freedom of worship, the Puritans thought that everyone in the colonies should worship the same way they did. Because there were so many of them, the Puritans controlled the government in much of New England. They were the only ones allowed to vote, and they passed very strict laws. Lawbreakers received harsh punishments. For example, someone caught lying might be forced to stand in the town square for hours locked in a pillory—wooden boards with holes cut in them for the head and hands. For other minor offenses, the offender was tied to a whipping post and given several lashes with a whip.

Except in cases of extreme illness, everyone in the New England colonies had to attend church on Sunday. The minister stood in a pulpit high above the pews to deliver his sermon, which could last four or five hours. The people sat on hard, straight-backed pews. In the winter, there was no heat, so church members brought foot warmers from home to use during the long services. In many churches, a "tithingman" walked up and down the aisles carrying a long stick. On one end there were feathers attached; the other end had a knob. If anyone dozed off, the tithingman would tickle him or her with the feathers. If this did not rouse the offender, he would thump them soundly with the knob.

Directions: Answer these questions about religion in the colonies.

1. The main idea is:

   ☐ Many New England colonists had come to America for religious freedom, and religion was very important to them.

   ☐ One of the first buildings erected in any new settlement was a church.

2. Which religious group exercised a lot of power in the New England colonies?

   _____

3. What was a pillory? _____

4. What was the only acceptable excuse for missing Sunday church services in the New England colonies? _____

5. What was the job of the tithingman? _____

Writing: Problem and Solution

Directions: Follow the instructions below.

1. Think of a problem the Colonial Americans may have encountered. Write a paragraph about this problem. In the paragraph, be sure to state the problem, then discuss why it would have been a problem for the colonists.

   _____

   _____

   _____

   _____

   _____

   _____

2. Think about a solution to the problem above. Write a paragraph outlining your ideas for the solution. Remember to state the solution to the problem and then your ideas to solve the problem.

   _____

   _____

   _____

   _____

   _____

   _____

Writing: Problem and Solution

Directions: Write a two-paragraph personal narrative about a problem you are experiencing. In the first paragraph, state reasons why it is a problem. In the second paragraph, write a possible solution to your problem.

_____

_____

_____

_____

_____

_____

_____

_____

_____

_____

Directions: Think of anything that could go wrong with your solution. Write about it below.

_____

_____

_____

_____

_____

_____

_____

Review

Many great colonists made an impact on American history. Among them was Benjamin Franklin, who left his mark as a printer, author, inventor, scientist and statesman. He has been called "the wisest American."

Franklin was born in Boston in 1706, one of 13 children in a very religious Puritan household. Although he had less than two years of formal education, his tremendous appetite for books served him well. At age 12, he became an apprentice printer at *The New England Courant* and soon began writing articles that poked fun at Boston society.

In 1723, Franklin ran away to Philadelphia, where he started his own newspaper. He was very active in the Philadelphia community. He operated a bookstore and was named postmaster. He also helped to establish a library, a fire company, a college, an insurance company and a hospital. His well-known *Poor Richard's Almanac* was first printed in 1732.

Over the years, Franklin maintained an interest in science and mechanics, leading to such inventions as a fireplace stove and bifocal lenses. In 1752, he gained world fame with his kite-and-key experiment, which proved that lightning was a form of electricity.

Franklin was an active supporter of the colonies throughout the Revolutionary War. He helped to write and was a signer of the Declaration of Independence in 1776. In his later years, he skillfully represented America in Europe, helping to work out a peace treaty with Great Britain.

Directions: Answer these questions about Benjamin Franklin.

1. The main idea is:

   ☐ Many great colonists made an impact on American history.

   ☐ Benjamin Franklin was a great colonist who left his mark as a printer, author, inventor, scientist and statesman.

2. How did Benjamin Franklin gain world fame? _____

3. What did Franklin sign and help to write? _____

4. Number in order the following accomplishments of Benjamin Franklin.

   _____ Served as representative of America in Europe

   _____ Began printing *Poor Richard's Almanac*

   _____ Experimented with electricity

   _____ Started his own newspaper

   _____ Helped to write and sign the Declaration of Independence

   _____ Served as apprentice printer on *The New England Courant*

Review

Directions: Match each item with its description. If necessary, review the section on colonial times.

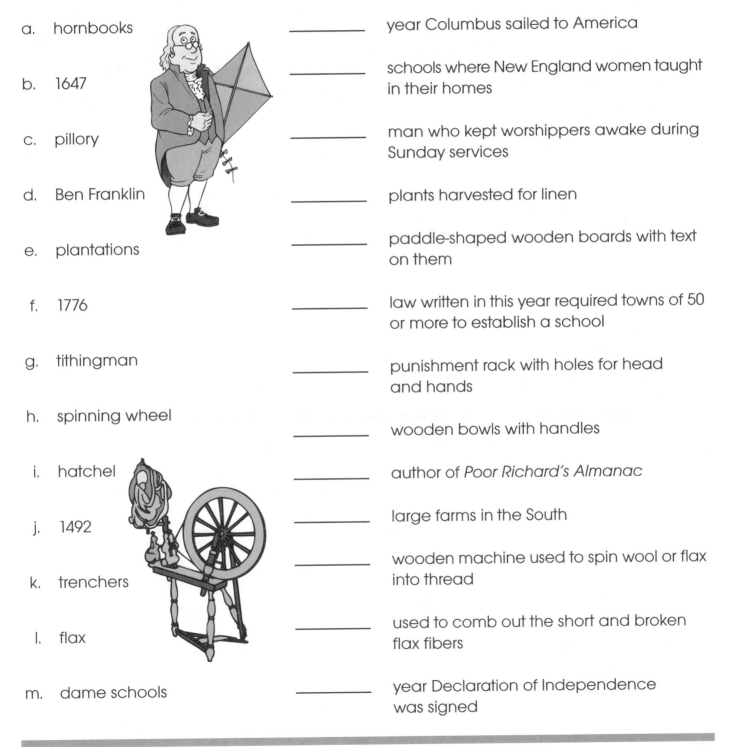

a. hornbooks

b. 1647

c. pillory

d. Ben Franklin

e. plantations

f. 1776

g. tithingman

h. spinning wheel

i. hatchel

j. 1492

k. trenchers

l. flax

m. dame schools

_____ year Columbus sailed to America

_____ schools where New England women taught in their homes

_____ man who kept worshippers awake during Sunday services

_____ plants harvested for linen

_____ paddle-shaped wooden boards with text on them

_____ law written in this year required towns of 50 or more to establish a school

_____ punishment rack with holes for head and hands

_____ wooden bowls with handles

_____ author of *Poor Richard's Almanac*

_____ large farms in the South

_____ wooden machine used to spin wool or flax into thread

_____ used to comb out the short and broken flax fibers

_____ year Declaration of Independence was signed

Recalling Details: The Earth's Atmosphere

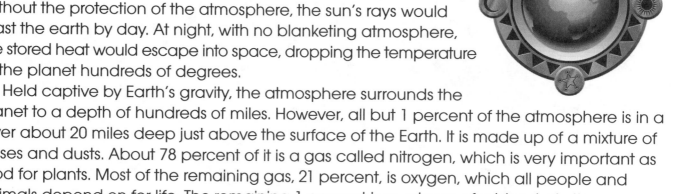

The most important reason that life can exist on Earth is its atmosphere—the air around us. Without it, plant and animal life could not have developed. There would be no clouds, weather or even sounds, only a deathlike stillness and an endlessly black sky. Without the protection of the atmosphere, the sun's rays would roast the earth by day. At night, with no blanketing atmosphere, the stored heat would escape into space, dropping the temperature of the planet hundreds of degrees.

Held captive by Earth's gravity, the atmosphere surrounds the planet to a depth of hundreds of miles. However, all but 1 percent of the atmosphere is in a layer about 20 miles deep just above the surface of the Earth. It is made up of a mixture of gases and dusts. About 78 percent of it is a gas called nitrogen, which is very important as food for plants. Most of the remaining gas, 21 percent, is oxygen, which all people and animals depend on for life. The remaining 1 percent is made up of a blend of other gases—including carbon dioxide, argon, ozone and helium—and tiny dust particles. These particles come from ocean salt crystals, bits of rocks and sand, plant pollen, volcanic ash and even meteor dust.

You may not think of air as matter, as something that can be weighed. In fact, the Earth's air weighs billions and billions of tons. Near the surface of the planet, this "air pressure" is greatest. Right now, about 10 tons of air is pressing in on you. Yet, like the fish living near the floor of the ocean, you don't notice this tremendous weight because your body is built to withstand it.

Directions: Answer these questions about the Earth's atmosphere.

1. What is the atmosphere? _____

2. Of what is the atmosphere made? _____

3. What is the most abundant gas in the atmosphere? _____

4. Which of the atmosphere's gases is most important to humans and animals?

    _____

5. What is air pressure? _____

Name: _____

Comprehension: Causes/Effects of Weather

The behavior of the atmosphere, which we experience as weather and climate, affects our lives in many important ways. It is the reason no one lives on the South Pole. It controls when a farmer plants the food we will eat, which crops will be planted and also whether those crops will grow. The weather tells you what clothes to wear and how you will play after school. Weather is the sum of all the conditions of the air that may affect the Earth's surface and its living things. These conditions include the temperature, air pressure, wind and moisture. Climate refers to these conditions but generally applies to larger areas and longer periods of time, such as the annual climate of South America rather than today's weather in Oklahoma City.

Climate is influenced by many factors. It depends first and foremost on latitude. Areas nearest the equator are warm and wet, while the poles are cold and relatively dry. The poles also have extreme seasonal changes, while the areas at the middle latitudes have more moderate climates, neither as cold as the poles nor as hot as the equator. Other circumstances may alter this pattern, however. Land near the oceans, for instance, is generally warmer than inland areas.

Elevation also plays a role in climate. For example, despite the fact that Africa's highest mountain, Kilimanjaro, is just south of the equator, its summit is perpetually covered by snow. In general, high land is cooler and wetter than nearby low land.

Directions: Check the answers to these questions about the causes and effects of weather.

1. What is the correct definition for **atmosphere**?

    ☐ the clouds   ☐ the sky   ☐ where weather occurs

2. What is the correct definition for **foremost**?

    ☐ most important   ☐ highest number   ☐ in the front

3. What is the correct definition for **circumstances**?

    ☐ temperatures   ☐ seasons   ☐ conditions

4. What is the correct definition for **elevation**?

    ☐ height above Earth   ☐ nearness to equator   ☐ snow covering

5. What is the correct definition for **perpetually**?

    ☐ occasionally   ☐ rarely   ☐ always

Name: _____

Main Idea/Recalling Details: Weather

People have always searched the sky for clues about upcoming weather. Throughout the ages, farmers and sailors have looked to the winds and clouds for signs of approaching storms. But no real understanding of the weather could be achieved without a scientific study of the atmosphere. Such a study depends on being able to measure certain conditions, including pressure, temperature and moisture levels.

A true scientific examination of weather, therefore, was not possible until the development of accurate measuring instruments, beginning in the 17th century. Meteorology—the science of studying the atmosphere—was born in 1643 with the invention of the barometer, which measures atmospheric pressure. The liquid-in-glass thermometer, the hygrometer to measure humidity—the mount of moisture in the air—and the weather map also were invented during the 1600s.

With the measurement of these basic elements, scientists began to work out the relationships between these and other atmospheric conditions, such as wind, clouds and rainfall. Still, their observations failed to show an overall picture of the weather. Such complete weather reporting had to wait two centuries for the rapid transfer of information made possible by the invention of the telegraph during the 1840s.

Today, the forecasts of meteorologists are an international effort. There are thousands of weather stations around the world, both at land and at sea. Upper-level observations are also made by weather balloons and satellites, which continuously send photographs back to earth. All of this information is relayed to national weather bureaus, where meteorologists plot it on graphs and analyze it. The information is then given to the public through newspapers and television and radio stations.

Directions: Answer these questions about studying the weather.

1. The main idea is:

☐ People have always searched the sky for clues about upcoming weather.
☐ A real understanding of weather depends on measuring conditions such as pressure, temperature and moisture levels.

2. List three kinds of instruments used to measure atmospheric conditions, and tell what conditions they measure.

1) _____   _____
2) _____   _____
3) _____   _____

3. During what century were many of these measuring instruments invented? _____

4. Name two things used for upper-level observations.

1) _____   2) _____

Name: _____

Comprehension: Hurricanes

The characteristics of a hurricane are powerful winds, driving rain and raging seas. Although a storm must have winds blowing at least 74 miles an hour to be classified as a hurricane, it is not unusual to have winds above 150 miles per hour. The entire storm system can be 500 miles in diameter, with lines of clouds that spiral toward a center called the "eye." Within the eye itself, which is about 15 miles across, the air is actually calm and cloudless. But this eye is enclosed by a towering wall of thick clouds where the storm's heaviest rains and highest winds are found.

All hurricanes begin in the warm seas and moist winds of the tropics. They form in either of two narrow bands to the north and south of the equator. For weeks, the blistering sun beats down on the ocean water. Slowly, the air above the sea becomes heated and begins to swirl. More hot, moist air is pulled skyward. Gradually, this circle grows larger and spins faster. As the hot, moist air at the top is cooled, great rain clouds are formed. The storm's fury builds until it moves over land or a cold area of the ocean where its supply of heat and moisture is finally cut off.

Hurricanes that strike North America usually form over the Atlantic Ocean. West coast storms are less dangerous because they tend to head out over the Pacific Ocean rather than toward land. The greatest damage usually comes from the hurricanes that begin in the western Pacific, because they often batter heavily populated regions.

Directions: Answer these questions about hurricanes.

1. What is necessary for a storm to be classified as a hurricane? _____

    _____

2. What is the "eye" of the hurricane? _____

3. Where do hurricanes come from? _____

4. How does a hurricane finally die down? _____

    _____

5. Why do hurricanes formed in the western Pacific cause the most damage?

    _____

Comprehension: Tornadoes

Tornadoes, which are also called twisters, occur more frequently than hurricanes, but they are smaller storms. The zigzag path of a tornado averages about 16 miles in length and only about a quarter of a mile wide. But the tornado is, pound for pound, the more severe storm. When one touches the ground, it leaves a trail of total destruction.

The winds in a tornado average about 200 miles per hour. At the center of the funnel-shaped cloud of a tornado is a partial vacuum. In combination with the high winds, this is what makes the storm so destructive. Its force is so great that a tornado can drive a piece of straw into a tree. The extremely low atmospheric pressure that accompanies the storm can cause a building to actually explode.

Unlike hurricanes, tornadoes are formed over land. They are most likely to occur over the central plains of the United States, especially in the spring and early summer months. Conditions for a tornado arise when warm, moist air from the south becomes trapped under colder, heavier air from the north. When the surfaces of the two air masses touch, rain clouds form and a thunderstorm begins. At first, only a rounded bulge hangs from the bottom of the cloud. It gradually gets longer until it forms a column reaching toward the ground. The tornado is white from the moisture when it first forms, but turns black as it sucks up dirt and trash.

Directions: Circle **True** or **False** for these statements about tornadoes.

1. The tornado is a stronger storm than the hurricane.   True   False

2. The path of a tornado usually covers hundreds of miles.   True   False

3. Like the eye of a hurricane, the center of a tornado is calm.   True   False

4. Tornadoes are most likely to occur in the central plains of the United States during the spring and early summer months.   True   False

5. High atmospheric pressure usually accompanies a tornado.   True   False

Comprehension: Thunderstorms

With warm weather comes the threat of thunderstorms. The rapid growth of the majestic thunderhead cloud and the damp, cool winds that warn of an approaching storm are familiar in most regions of the world. In fact, it has been estimated that at any given time 1,800 such storms are in progress around the globe.

As with hurricanes and tornadoes, thunderstorms are formed when a warm, moist air mass meets with a cold air mass. Before long, bolts of lightning streak across the sky, and thunder booms. It is not entirely understood how lightning is formed. It is known that a positive electrical charge builds near the top of the cloud, and a negative charge forms at the bottom. When enough force builds up, a powerful current of electricity zigzags down an electrically charged pathway between the two, causing the flash of lightning.

The clap of thunder you hear after a lightning flash is created by rapidly heated air that expands as the lightning passes through it. The distant rumbling is caused by the thunder's sound waves bouncing back and forth within clouds or between mountains. When thunderstorms rumble through an area, many people begin to worry about tornadoes. But they need to be just as fearful of thunderstorms. In fact, lightning kills more people than any other severe weather condition. In 1988, lightning killed 68 people in the United States, while tornadoes killed 32.

Directions: Answer these questions about thunderstorms.

1. How many thunderstorms are estimated to be occurring at any given time around the world?

   _____

2. When are thunderstorms formed?

   _____

3. What causes thunder?

   _____

4. On average, which causes more deaths, lightning or tornadoes?

   _____

READING 6

Venn Diagram: Storms

Directions: Complete the Venn diagram below. Think of at least three things to write in the outer parts of each circle and at least three things to write in the intersecting parts.

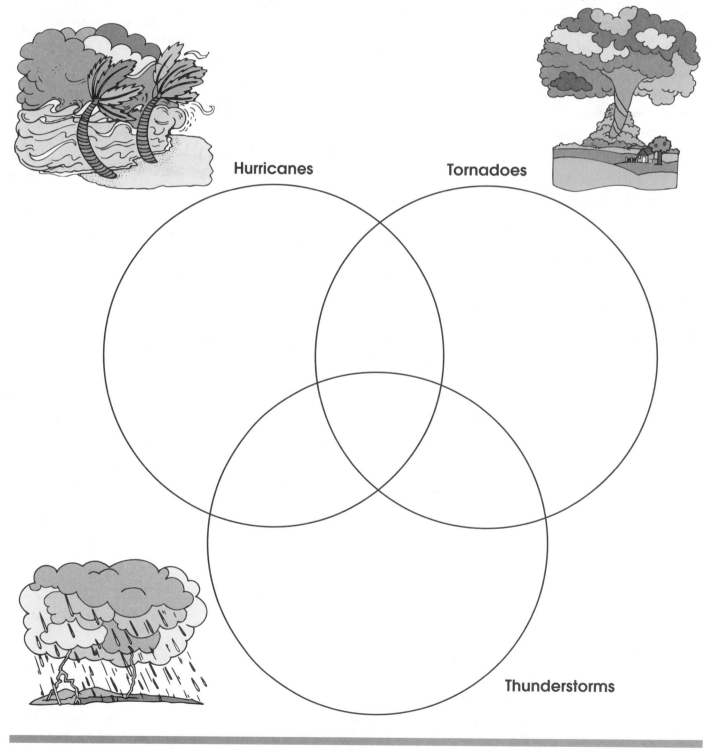

Hurricanes

Tornadoes

Thunderstorms

Writing: Weather

Directions: Write an essay about your own experience in a severe storm. Write at least three paragraphs, and include the following:

What type of storm was it?
Where were you?
How did you feel?

_____

_____

_____

_____

_____

_____

_____

_____

_____

_____

_____

_____

Writing Checklist

Reread your essay carefully.

☐ My essay makes sense.   ☐ I have a good opening and ending.

☐ There are no jumps in ideas.   ☐ I used correct spelling.

☐ I used correct punctuation.   ☐ My essay is well-organized.

☐ My essay is interesting.

Name: _____

Recalling Details: Lightning Safety Rules

Lightning causes more fire damage to forests and property than anything else. More importantly, it kills more people than any other weather event. It is important to know what to do—and what not to do—during a thunderstorm. Here are some important rules to remember:

- **Don't** go outdoors.

- **Don't** go near open doors or windows, fireplaces, radiators, stoves, metal pipes, sinks or plug-in electrical appliances.

- **Don't** use the telephone, as lightning could strike the wires outside.

- **Don't** handle metal objects, such as fishing poles or golf clubs.

- **Don't** go into the water or ride in small boats.

- **Do** stay in an automobile if you are traveling. Cars offer excellent protection.

- **Don't** take laundry off the clothesline.

- **Do** look for shelter if you are outdoors. If there is no shelter, stay away from the highest object in the area. If there are only a few trees nearby, it is best to crouch in the open, away from the trees at a distance greater than the height of the nearest tree. If you are in an area with many trees, avoid the tallest tree. Look for shorter ones.

- **Don't** take shelter near wire fences or clotheslines, exposed sheds or on a hilltop.

- If your hair stands on end or your skin tingles, lightning may be about to strike you. Immediately crouch down, put your feet together and place your hands over your ears.

Directions: Answer these questions about lightning safety rules.

1. Name two things you should avoid if you are looking for shelter outside.

    1) _____

    2) _____

2. What should you do if, during a thunderstorm, your hair stands up or your skin tingles?

    _____

    _____

Main Idea/Comprehension: Rainbows

Although there are some violent, frightening aspects of the weather, there is, of course, considerable beauty, too. The rainbow is one simple, lovely example of nature's atmospheric mysteries.

You usually can see a rainbow when the sun comes out after a rain shower or in the fine spray of a waterfall or fountain. Although sunlight appears to be white, it is actually made up of a mixture of colors—all the colors in the rainbow. We see a rainbow because thousands of tiny raindrops act as mirrors and prisms on the sunlight. Prisms are objects that bend light, splitting it into bands of color.

The bands of color form a perfect semicircle. From the top edge to the bottom, the colors are always in the same order—red, orange, yellow, green, indigo and violet. The brightness and width of each band may vary from one minute to the next. You also may notice that the sky framed by the rainbow is lighter than the sky above. This is because the light that forms the blue and violet bands is more bent and spread out than the light that forms the top red band.

You will always see morning rainbows in the west, with the sun behind you. Afternoon rainbows, likewise, are always in the east. To see a rainbow, the sun can be no higher than 42 degrees—nearly halfway up the sky. Sometimes, if the sunlight is strong and the water droplets are very small, you can see a double rainbow. This happens because the light is reflected twice in the water droplets. The color bands are fainter and in reverse order in the second band.

Directions: Answer these questions about rainbows.

1. Check the statement that is the main idea.

   ☐ Although there are violent, frightening aspects of weather, there is considerable beauty, too.

   ☐ The rainbow is one simple, lovely example of nature's atmospheric mysteries.

2. What is the correct definition for **semicircle**?

   ☐ colored circle   ☐ diameter of a circle   ☐ half circle

3. What is a prism? _____

4. In which direction would you look to see an afternoon rainbow? _____

Name: _____

Comprehension: Cause and Effect

Directions: Complete the chart by listing the cause and effect of each weather phenomenon.

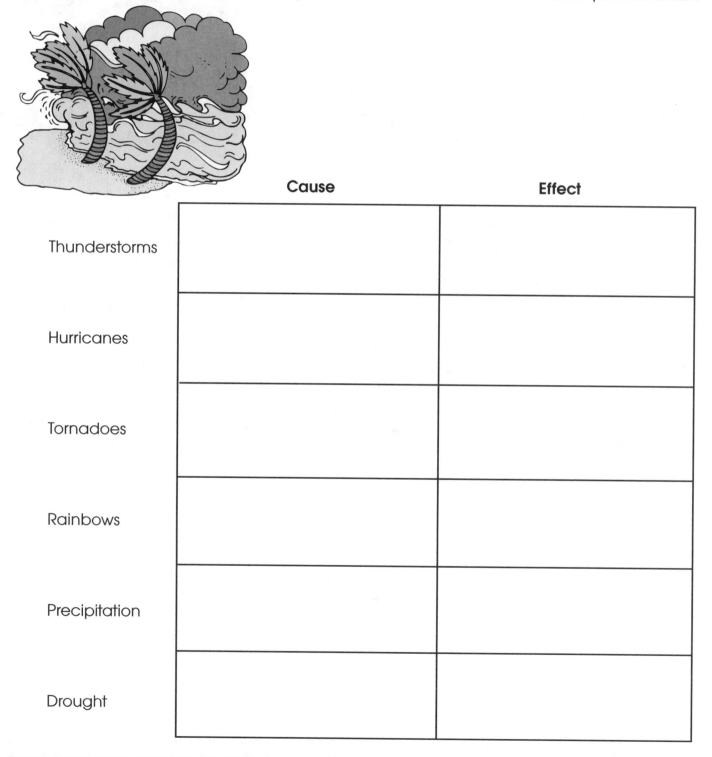

	Cause	Effect
Thunderstorms		
Hurricanes		
Tornadoes		
Rainbows		
Precipitation		
Drought		

Name: _____

Review

Directions: If necessary, review the section on weather to find the answers to the following questions.

1. Describe the earth's atmosphere. _____

_____

2. The science of studying weather is called _____ .

3. Why is it important for weather forecasting to be an international effort?

_____

_____

_____

4. Define **weather**. _____

_____

5. Name three factors that influence climate.

_____ _____ _____

6. Describe the following weather phenomena.

a. hurricane _____

_____

b. tornado _____

_____

c. thunderstorm _____

_____

Name: _____

Review

Directions: If necessary, review the section on weather to find answers to the following questions.

1. What atmospheric conditions are necessary for a tornado to form?

    _____

2. Describe how scientists believe lightning is formed.

    _____

    _____

    _____

3. How is a rainbow formed?

    _____

4. Research a famous hurricane, such as Iniki or Andrew. Write an informational paragraph about it.

    _____

    _____

    _____

    _____

Writing Checklist

Reread your paragraph carefully.

☐ My paragraph makes sense.   ☐ I have a good opening and ending.

☐ I used correct punctuation.   ☐ I used correct spelling.

☐ There are no jumps in ideas.   ☐ My paragraph is well-organized.

☐ My paragraph is interesting.

Name: _____

Recalling Details: The Island Continent

Australia is the only country that fills an entire continent. It is the smallest continent in the world but the sixth largest country. Australia, called the island continent, is totally surrounded by water—the Indian Ocean on the west and south, the Pacific Ocean on the east and the Arafura Sea, which is formed by these two oceans coming together, to the north.

The island continent is, in large part, a very dry, flat land. Yet it supports a magnificent and unusual collection of wildlife. Because of its remoteness, Australia is home to plants and animals that are not found anywhere else in the world. Besides the well-known kangaroo and koala, the strange animals of the continent include the wombat, dingo, kookaburra, emu and, perhaps the strangest of all, the duckbill platypus.

There are many physical features of Australia that also are unique, including the central part of the country known as the "Outback," which consists of three main deserts—the Great Sandy, the Gibson and the Great Victoria. Because much of the country is desert, more than half of all Australians live in large, modern cities along the coast. There are also many people living in the small towns on the edge of the Outback, where there is plenty of grass for raising sheep and cattle. Australia rates first in the world for sheep raising. In fact, there are more than 10 times as many sheep in Australia as there are people!

Directions: Answer these questions about Australia.

1. What are the three large bodies of water that surround Australia?

    1) _____ 2) _____ 3) _____

2. Besides the kangaroo and the koala, name three other unusual animals found only in Australia.

    1) _____ 2) _____ 3) _____

3. What three deserts make up the "Outback?"

    1) _____ 2) _____ 3) _____

Name: _____

Comprehension: The Aborigines

The native, or earliest known, people of Australia are the Aborigines (ab-ur-IJ-uh-neez). They arrived on the continent from Asia more than 20,000 years ago. Before the Europeans began settling in Australia during the early 1800s, there were about 300,000 Aborigines. But the new settlers brought diseases that killed many of these native people. Today there are only about 125,000 Aborigines living in Australia, many of whom now live in the cities.

The way of life of the Aborigines, who still live like their ancestors, is closely related to nature. They live as hunters and gatherers and do not produce crops or raise livestock. The Aborigines have no permanent settlements, only small camps near watering places. Because they live off the land, they must frequently move about in search of food. They have few belongings and little or no clothing.

Some tribes of Aborigines, especially those that live in the desert, may move 100 times in a year. They might move more than 1,000 miles on foot during that time. These tribes set up temporary homes, such as tents made of bark and igloo-like structures made of grass.

The Aborigines have no written language, but they have developed a system of hand signals. These are used during hunting when silence is necessary and during their elaborate religious ceremonies when talking is forbidden.

Directions: Circle **True** or **False** for these statements about Aborigines.

1. The Aborigines came from Europe to settle in Australia.   True   False

2. The Aborigines live as hunters and gatherers rather than as farmers.   True   False

3. The tribes move about often to find jobs.   True   False

4. The people move often to help them raise their livestock.   True   False

5. Aborigine tribes always move 200 times a year.   True   False

Name: _____

Main Idea/Comprehension: The Boomerang

The Aborigines have developed a few tools and weapons, including spears, flint knives and the boomerang. The boomerang comes in different shapes and has many uses. This curved throwing stick is used for hunting, playing, digging, cutting and even making music.

You may have seen a boomerang that, when thrown, returns to the thrower. This type of boomerang is sometimes used in duck hunting, but it is most often used as a toy and for sporting contests. It is lightweight—about three-fourths of a pound—and has a big curve in it. However, the boomerang used by the Aborigines for hunting is much heavier and is nearly straight. It does not return to its thrower.

Because of its sharp edges, the boomerang makes a good knife for skinning animals. The Aborigines also use boomerangs as digging sticks, to sharpen stone blades, to start fires and as swords and clubs in fighting. Boomerangs sometimes are used to make music—two clapped together provide rhythmic background for dances. Some make musical sounds when they are pulled across one another.

To throw a boomerang, the thrower grasps it at one end and holds it behind his head. He throws it overhanded, adding a sharp flick of the wrist at the last moment. It is thrown into the wind to make it come back. A skillful thrower can do many tricks with his boomerang. He can make it spin in several circles, or make a figure eight in the air. He can even make it bounce on the ground several times before it soars into the air and returns.

Directions: Answer these questions about boomerangs.

1. The main idea is:

   ☐ The Aborigines have developed a few tools and weapons, including spears, flint knives and the boomerang.

   ☐ The boomerang comes in different shapes and has many uses.

2. To make it return, the thrower tosses the boomerang

   ☐ into the wind.   ☐ against the wind.

3. List three uses for the boomerang.

   1) _____

   2) _____

   3) _____

Name: _____

Comprehension: The Kangaroo

Many animals found in Australia are not found anywhere else in the world. Because the island continent was separated from the rest of the world for many years, these animals developed in different ways. Many of the animals in Australia are marsupials. Marsupials are animals whose babies are born underdeveloped and are then carried in a pouch on the mother's body until they are able to care for themselves. The kangaroo is perhaps the best known of the marsupials.

There are 45 kinds of kangaroos, and they come in a variety of sizes. The smallest is the musky rat kangaroo, which is about a foot long, including its hairless tail. It weighs only a pound. The largest is the gray kangaroo, which is more than 9 feet long, counting its tail, and can weigh 200 pounds. When moving quickly, a kangaroo can leap 25 feet and move at 30 miles an hour!

A baby kangaroo, called a joey, is totally helpless at birth. It is only three-quarters of an inch long and weighs but a fraction of an ounce. The newly born joey immediately crawls into its mother's pouch and remains there until it is old enough to be independent—which can be as long as eight months.

Kangaroos eat grasses and plants. They can cause problems for farmers and ranchers in Australia because they compete with cattle for pastures. During a drought, kangaroos may invade ranches and even airports looking for food.

Directions: Answer these questions about kangaroos.

1. What are marsupials? _____

    _____

2. What is the smallest kangaroo? _____

3. What is a baby kangaroo called? _____

4. Why did Australian animals develop differently from other animals? _____

    _____

Name: _____

Comprehension: The Koala

The koala lives in eastern Australia in the eucalyptus (you-ca-LIP-tes) forests. These slow, gentle animals hide by day, usually sleeping in the trees. They come out at night to eat. Koalas eat only certain types of eucalyptus leaves. Their entire way of life centers on this unique diet. The koala's digestive system is specially adapted for eating eucalyptus leaves. In fact, to other animals, these leaves are poisonous!

The wooly, round-eared koala looks like a cuddly teddy bear, but it is not related to any bear. It is a marsupial like the kangaroo. And, like the joey, a baby koala requires a lot of care. It will remain constantly in its mother's pouch until it is six months old. After that, a baby koala will ride piggyback on its mother for another month or two, even though it is nearly as big as she is. Koalas have few babies—only one every other year. While in her pouch, the baby koala lives on its mother's milk. After it is big enough to be on its own, the koala will almost never drink anything again.

Oddly, the mother koala's pouch is backwards—the opening is at the bottom. This leads scientists to believe that the koala once lived on the ground and walked on all fours. But at some point, the koala became a tree dweller. This makes an upside-down pouch very awkward! The babies keep from falling to the ground by holding on tightly with their mouths. The mother koala has developed strong muscles around the rim of her pouch that also help

Directions: Answer these questions about koalas.

1. What is the correct definition for **eucalyptus**?

□ enormous   □ a type of tree   □ rain

2. What is the correct definition for **digestive**?

□ the process in which food is absorbed in the body
□ the process of finding food
□ the process of tasting

3. What is the correct definition for **dweller**?

□ one who climbs   □ one who eats   □ one who lives in

Comprehension: The Wombat

Another animal unique to Australia is the wombat. The wombat has characteristics in common with other animals. Like the koala, the wombat is also a marsupial with a backwards pouch. The pouch is more practical for the wombat, which lives on the ground rather than in trees. The wombat walks on all fours so the baby is in less danger of falling out.

The wombat resembles a beaver without a tail. With its strong claws, it is an expert digger. It makes long tunnels beneath cliffs and boulders in which it sleeps all day. At night, it comes out to look for food. It has strong, beaver-like teeth to chew through the various plant roots it eats. A wombat's teeth have no roots, like a rodent's. Its teeth keep growing from the inside as they are worn down from the outside.

The wombat, which can be up to 4 feet long and weighs 60 pounds when full grown, eats only grass, plants and roots. It is a shy, quiet and gentle animal that would never attack. But when angered, it has a strong bite and very sharp teeth! And, while wombats don't eat or attack other animals, the many deep burrows they dig to sleep in are often dangerous to the other animals living nearby.

Directions: Answer these questions about the wombat.

1. How is the wombat similar to the koala? _____

   _____

2. How is the wombat similar to the beaver? _____

   _____

3. How is the wombat similar to a rodent? _____

   _____

   _____

Comprehension: The Duckbill Platypus

Australia's duckbill platypus is a most unusual animal. It is very strange-looking and has caused a lot of confusion for people studying it. For many years, even scientists did not know how to classify it. The platypus has webbed feet and a bill like a duck. But it doesn't have wings, has fur instead of feathers and has four legs instead of two. The baby platypus gets milk from its mother, like a mammal, but it is hatched from a tough-skinned egg, like a reptile. A platypus also has a poisonous spur on each of its back legs that is like the tip of a viper's fangs. Scientists have put the platypus—along with another strange animal from Australia called the spiny anteater—in a special class of mammal called "monotremes."

The platypus has an amazing appetite! It has been estimated that a full-grown platypus eats about 1,200 earthworms, 50 crayfish and numerous tadpoles and insects every day. The platypus is an excellent swimmer and diver. It dives under the water of a stream and searches the muddy bottom for food.

A mother platypus lays one or two eggs, which are very small—only about an inch long—and leathery in appearance. During the seven to 14 days it takes for the eggs to hatch, the mother never leaves them, not even to eat. The tiny platypus, which is only a half-inch long, cuts its way out of the shell with a sharp point on its bill. This point is known as an "egg tooth," and it will fall off soon after birth. (Many reptiles and birds have egg teeth, but they are unknown in other mammals.) By the time it is 4 months old, the baby platypus is about a foot long—half its adult size—and is learning how to swim and hunt.

Directions: Answer these questions about the duckbill platypus.

1. In what way is a duckbill platypus like other mammals? _____

_____

2. In what way is it like a reptile? _____

3. What other animal is in the class of mammal called "monotremes"?

_____

4. What makes up the diet of a platypus? _____

5. On what other animals would you see an "egg tooth"? _____

Name: _____

Recalling Details: Animals of Australia

Directions: Complete the chart with information from the selection on Australian animals.

	Gray Kangaroo	Koala	Wombat	Platypus
What are the animal's physical characteristics?				
What is the animal's habitat?				
What does the animal eat?				

Name:_____

Main Idea/Recalling Details: Land Down Under

Australia and New Zealand are often referred to as the "land down under." The name, made popular by American soldiers stationed there during World War II, grew out of the idea that these two countries are opposite or below Europe on the globe. While Australia and New Zealand are often linked, they are individual countries, separated by more than 1,000 miles of ocean.

Their landscapes are quite different. New Zealand is made up of two main islands, North and South Island, which are nearly covered by snowy mountains. One of the most unusual and beautiful areas of New Zealand is the volcanic region around Lake Taupo on North Island. There you will see boiling springs, pools of steaming mud, hot-water geysers, small lakes with beds of brightly colored rocks and waterfalls. While most of the people of New Zealand live and work in the industrialized cities, dairy farming is most important to the country's economy. The New Zealanders eat more meat and butter than people anywhere else in the world, and they sell huge amounts to other countries.

As in Australia, many of the customs in New Zealand would be familiar to a traveler from America because the two countries were settled by British settlers hundreds of years ago. However, the native islanders have descended from Asian ancestors, so the remnants of ancient Eastern practices exist alongside the European way of life.

Directions: Answer these questions about New Zealand and Australia.

1. The main idea is:

   ☐ Australia and New Zealand are often referred to as the "land down under."

   ☐ While Australia and New Zealand are often linked, they are individual countries.

2. What is the correct definition for **landscape**?

   ☐ natural scenery and features   ☐ mountainsides   ☐ natural resources

3. What is the correct definition for **economy**?

   ☐ thrifty   ☐ money management   ☐ countryside

4. What is the nickname for Australia and New Zealand? _____

5. What business is most important to the New Zealand economy? _____

Name: _____

Writing: Australia

Directions: Write a three-paragraph informational essay on Australia. Discuss the land, its native people and its animals.

_____

_____

_____

_____

_____

_____

_____

_____

_____

_____

_____

Writing Checklist

Reread your essay carefully.

☐ My essay makes sense.   ☐ I have a good opening and ending.

☐ There are no jumps in ideas.   ☐ I used correct spelling.

☐ I used correct punctuation.   ☐ My essay is well-organized.

☐ My essay is interesting.

Name: _____

Venn Diagrams: Australia and New Zealand

Directions: Although Australia and New Zealand are close geographically to each other, they have many differences. After reading the selection, "Land Down Under," complete the following Venn diagram.

Australia   **New Zealand**

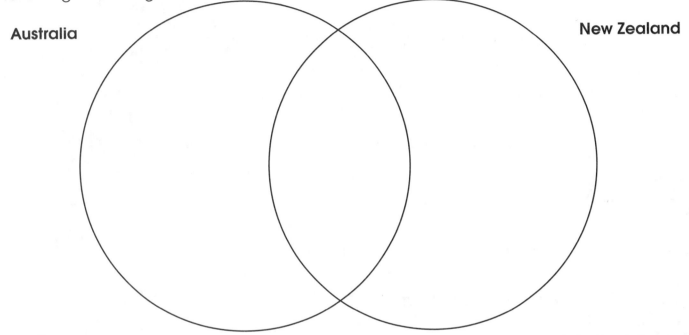

Directions: Using your knowledge of the United States and Australia, complete the following Venn diagram.

Australia   **United States**

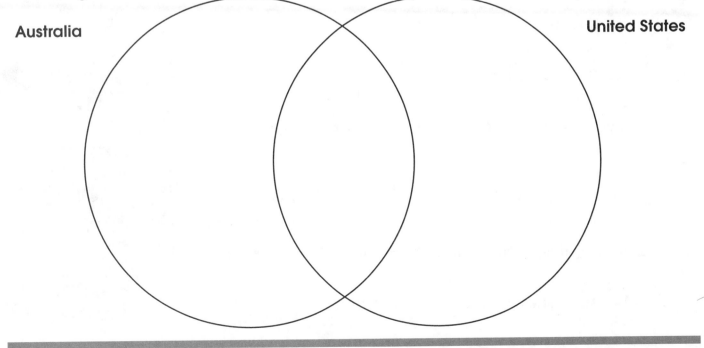

Review

Directions: Write **T** for true and **F** for false.

_____ 1. Australia and New Zealand are similar in landscape.

_____ 2. Australia is home to the duckbill platypus.

_____ 3. The wombat resembles a beaver without a tail.

_____ 4. The platypus is a special mammal called a monotreme.

_____ 5. A kangaroo is a marsupial.

_____ 6. Baby kangaroos are independent at birth.

_____ 7. Koalas are related to bears.

_____ 8. Female koalas and kangaroos both have pouches.

_____ 9. Koalas eat all types of leaves.

_____ 10. There are over 40 kinds of kangaroos.

_____ 11. The Australian Outback is located in the central part of the country.

_____ 12. Australia raises more sheep than any other country.

_____ 13. Aborigines arrived in Australia over 20,000 years ago.

_____ 14. Aborigines live in one central place.

Main Idea/Recalling Details: Kites

Kites are a familiar sight on breezy fall days. They come in a great variety of sizes, colors and designs. It is not known who invented kites, but kites have been flown since the beginning of recorded history. While today children and adults use them for recreation, throughout history kites have had other uses.

In the United States, kites have been used in weather and other scientific research experiments. Before airplanes and weather balloons, the National Weather Service had kites carry weather instruments as high as 4 miles above the earth. In addition, the United States military used kites for observing the enemy and sending messages between troops.

In other countries, kites had cultural and religious importance. The ancient Chinese flew kites over their homes to drive out evil spirits. The Chinese still enjoy kites so much that one day each year they celebrate Kites' Day.

On some Pacific islands, kites were thought to have spiritual qualities. They were believed to symbolize both sides of nature—life and death. On some Polynesian islands, kites were used as protection against evil. These kites were often shaped like birds and used as soaring messengers to the heavens. In Hawaii, kites were also used to establish land ownership. A kite was released in the air, and a claim was given for the area where it came down.

Directions: Answer these questions about kites.

1. The main idea is:

   ☐ Kites come in a great variety of sizes, color and designs.

   ☐ While today kites are used for recreation, throughout history they
      have had other uses.

2. Besides recreation, name two ways kites have been used in the United States.

   1) _____

   2) _____

3. What country celebrates a holiday called Kites' Day? _____

4. How did Hawaiians use kites to decide land ownership? _____

   _____

Name: _____

Comprehension: Aerodynamics

Kites are able to fly because of the principle of aerodynamics. This big word simply means the study of forces that are put into action by moving air. Three main forces work to keep a heavier-than-air kite flying—lift, gravity and drag.

This is how it works: The flying lines, or strings, are attached to the kite to hold it at a slant. The wind pushes against the underside of the kite. At the same time, the wind rushes around the edges of the kite and "drags" some of the air from the upper side. This creates a partial vacuum there. The push of the air underneath is greater than the push of the air from the top, so the kite is held in the air. An airplane is held in the air in much the same way, except that it must keep moving rapidly to make the pressure above and below its wings different. The wind does this for the kite. In a steady airstream, a kite doesn't move backward or forward. It seems to be unaffected by gravity. This is possible because the lifting force of the wind overcomes the downward force of gravity.

If you have ever ridden a bicycle into a strong wind, you may have felt some of the forces of aerodynamics. If you held your hand out to your side, you could feel the air stream flowing around your hand. With your fingers pointed into the wind and your hand held level, there is little lift or drag. But if you raised your fingers slightly, the wind lifted your hand upwards. Raising your hand higher increases the drag and decreases the lift. Your hand is pushed downward. A kite flying in the sky is subject to these same forces.

Directions: Answer these questions about aerodynamics.

1. What is aerodynamics? _____

_____

2. What three forces are at work to hold a kite in the air?

   1) _____ 2) _____ 3) _____

3. An airplane is held in the air in much the same way, except that it must keep moving rapidly to keep the air above and below its wings different.

   True   False

Name: _____

Comprehension: Getting Your Kite to Fly

There are some basic things to know about kite flying that can help you enjoy the sport more. Here are a few of the most important ones.

First, if you have ever seen someone flying a kite in a movie, you probably saw him or her get the kite off the ground by running into the wind. However, this is not the way to launch a kite. Most beginners will find a "high-start" launch to be the easiest. For a high-start launch, have a friend stand about 100 feet away, facing into the wind. Your friend should face you and hold the kite gently. Place some tension on the flying line by pulling gently on it. With a steady breeze behind you, tug gently on the line, and the kite will rise. If your kite begins to dive, don't panic or pull on the line. Dropping the reel will cause it to spin out of control and could cause someone to be hurt. Simply let the line go slack. This usually will right the kite in midair.

For a kite that is pulling hard away from you, have a friend stand behind you and take up the slack line as you bring it in. Hand over hand, pull down the kite. It is very important to have gloves on to do this, or you may burn or cut your hands. It is recommended that you always wear gloves while kite flying.

When two kite lines get crossed, pulling may cause enough friction to cut one or both of the lines. Instead of pulling, both fliers should walk toward one another until their lines uncross as they pass.

Directions: Circle **True** or **False** for these statements about kite flying.

1. To launch a kite, run into the wind holding the kite behind you.   True   False

2. In a high-start launch, a friend stands about 100 feet away from you, holding the kite.   True   False

3. If your kite begins to dive from the sky, immediately drop the reel.   True   False

4. It is recommended that you always wear gloves when kite flying.   True   False

Name: _____

Recalling Details: Kite Safety Rules

Because kite flying is a relaxed, easy-going sport, it is easy to have the mistaken belief that there are no dangers involved. However, like any sport, kite flying must be approached with care. Here are some important safety rules you should always follow while kite flying:

- **Don't** fly a kite in wet or stormy weather or use wet flying line.

- **Don't** fly a kite near electrical power lines, transmission towers or antennae. If your kite does get caught in one of these, walk away and leave it! If you must get the kite back, contact your local electric company.

- **Don't** use wire for flying line.

- **Don't** use metal for any part of the kite.

- **Don't** fly a kite near a street or in crowded areas.

- **Don't** fly a kite in a field or other area that has rocks or other objects you could trip over.

- **Don't** walk backwards without looking behind you.

- **Don't** fly a kite around trees. (If your kite does happen to get caught in a tree, let the line go slack. Sometimes the wind can work it free.)

- **Don't** fly a kite using unfamiliar equipment. A reel spinning out of control can be quite dangerous.

- **Don't** fly a kite near an airport.

- **Don't** fly a very large kite without proper guidance.

- **Do** wear protective gloves to avoid burns on your hands from rapidly unwinding line.

- **Do** use flying line that has been tested for the type and size of kite you are using.

Directions: Answer these questions about kite safety.

1. List three things you should never fly a kite around.

   1) _____ 2) _____ 3) _____

2. What should you do if your kite gets caught in a tree? _____

   _____

3. What material should you never use in any part of your kite? _____

Name: _____

Recalling Details: Aviation Pioneer

Lawrence Hargrave was born in Middlesex, England, in 1850. When he was a teenager, his family moved to Australia. There Hargrave went to work for the Australian Stream and Navigation Company, where he spent 5 years gaining practical experience in engineering. He soon became interested in artificial flight.

Hargrave wanted to develop a stable lifting surface that could be used for flying. This goal led to his invention of the box kite, one of the seven basic models. In 1894, he carried out kite experiments along the beaches near his home. One day, in front of onlookers, he was lifted above the beach and out over the sea by four of his box kites. These experiments were very important to the development of air travel, although Hargrave has received little credit for it. In fact, because of his modesty, Hargrave failed to get a patent on his box kite. He spent more than 30 years studying flying, offering many inventions, including a rotary engine.

In 1906, Hargrave began looking for a home for his collection of nearly 200 models of kites and flying machines. After being rejected by several governments, his collection was accepted at a technological museum in Munich, Germany. Unfortunately, many of these models were destroyed during World War I.

Directions: Answer these questions about Lawrence Hargrave.

1. For what kite design was Lawrence Hargrave known? _____

2. What was Hargrave trying to create when he made this kite?

   _____

3. What was one of the inventions Hargrave contributed to aviation? _____

   _____

4. Where was Hargrave's collection of kites and flying machines finally housed?

   _____

Name: _____

Main Idea/Recalling Details: A Kite in History

In June 1752, Benjamin Franklin proved that lightning was a type of electricity by flying a kite with a key tied to the bottom of the line during a thunderstorm. Before his experiment, many people thought that lightning was a supernatural power.

After the success of his experiment, Franklin figured that if lightning could be drawn to a kite in a storm, it could be safely redirected into the ground by a metal rod attached to a house. His idea was met with much doubt, but lightning rods were soon seen on buildings in many of the colonies and later in Europe. During the years between 1683 and 1789, studying the universe and laws of nature was of tremendous importance. It was during this Age of Reason, as it was known, that Franklin's kite experiment gained him international fame and respect. He was elected to the Royal Society of London and the French Academy of Sciences, among other honors.

More than 20 years after his bold experiment, American patriots were enduring many hardships in their struggles for freedom from England. The colonial troops had shortages of guns, gun powder and food. France was sending supplies but not as much as was needed. Benjamin Franklin was chosen to go to France to persuade the French to aid the American cause. Franklin's reputation as a brilliant scientist earned him a hero's welcome there. The French people were so impressed by him that they wanted to help the colonies, even during a time when they could barely afford it. The supplies sent by the French were instrumental to the colonists in winning the war. And it all started with a kite.

Directions: Answer these questions about Ben Franklin and his historical kite.

1. The main idea is:

   ☐ A kite played a role in the American Revolution and gained a spot in history books.

   ☐ Benjamin Franklin proved that lightning was a type of electricity by flying a kite with a key tied to the bottom of the line during a storm.

2. From his kite and key experiment, what did Franklin invent? _____

3. What was the era between 1683 and 1789 known as? _____

4. Why was Franklin sent to France in 1776? _____

_____

Summarizing: Pioneers

Directions: Think about the lives and accomplishments of Ben Franklin and Lawrence Hargrave. Write one paragraph about each, summarizing what you have learned about these two men.

Ben Franklin

_____

_____

_____

_____

_____

Lawrence Hargrave

_____

_____

_____

_____

_____

Writing Checklist
Reread your paragraphs carefully.

☐ My paragraphs make sense.　　☐ I used correct spelling.

☐ I used correct punctuation.　　☐ My paragraphs are well-organized.

☐ I have a good opening and ending.　　☐ My paragraphs are interesting.

Review

Directions: Number in order the steps for how to launch a kite.

_____ With a steady breeze behind you, gently pull on the line.

_____ Have your friend face you and gently hold the kite.

_____ Your kite will rise.

_____ Have your friend face into the wind.

_____ Place some tension on the flying line by pulling on it.

_____ Have a friend stand about 100 feet away from you.

Directions: Write **True** or **False** for these statements about kite safety.

_____ 1. You should not use wire for flying line.

_____ 2. Fly any size kite you wish as long as you have the right flying line.

_____ 3. If your kite gets caught in a tree, let the line go slack.

_____ 4. It's okay to fly a kite in the rain.

_____ 5. You should not fly a kite in crowded areas.

_____ 6. You can use metal on your kite as long as it's not the flying line itself.

_____ 7. You don't need to wear gloves unless you're flying a very large kite.

_____ 8. You should not fly a kite around an airport.

_____ 9. If your kite gets caught in power lines, just tug the line gently until it works free.

_____ 10. The best place to fly a kite is in a large field.

Name: _____

Review

Directions: Answer these questions about kites.

1. In a paragraph, describe how a kite works.

   _____

   _____

   _____

   _____

   _____

   _____

2. Define **aerodynamics**.

   _____

   _____

3. Describe how to launch a kite.

   _____

   _____

   _____

4. List two accomplishments of each man.

   Lawrence Hargrave

   1) _____

   2) _____

   Benjamin Franklin

   1) _____

   2) _____

5. Write **F** for fact and **O** for opinion.

   _____ Kite flying is a sport only children enjoy.

   _____ In a steady wind, kites appear to be unaffected by gravity.

   _____ Kites are for enjoyment only.

Name: _____

Cumulative Review

Directions: Follow the instructions below.

1. Add a prefix from the box to the following words.
   Then write a definition for that word.

extra	inter	sub	trans	pre

   title _____

   _____

   exist _____

   _____

   continental _____

   _____

   terrestrial _____

   _____

   connect _____

   _____

2. Add a suffix from the box to the following words.
   Then write a definition for that word.

ance	ous	an	ship	ment

   enjoy _____

   _____

   citizen _____

   _____

Name: _____

Cumulative Review

Africa _____

_____

mischief _____

_____

perform _____

_____

3. Write the correct definition for the bold homograph.

Use a **minute** amount of detergent in that machine.

_____

I'll have to **resort** to using my allowance to make the purchase.

_____

Contracts are used in most business agreements.

_____

4. Write **M** if the sentence contains a metaphor. Write **S** if it contains a simile.

_____ Waves hit the beach like a thousand hammers.

_____ He runs like the wind.

_____ I am a turtle when it comes to finishing a project.

_____ She was as quiet as a mouse creeping up behind him.

_____ The young child's hair was spun gold in the sunlight.

5. The following sentence demonstrates what figure of speech? _____

The fight they had was soon water under the bridge.

6. A word's _____ is its exact meaning.

A word's _____ is the idea associated with the word.

Name: _____

Cumulative Review

7. Complete the analogies.

attract : repel :: entertain : _____

finger : hand :: toe : _____

frog : leap :: cheetah : _____

carton : box :: couch : _____

8. Draw an **X** through the item that does not belong and replace it with one that does belong.

cheetah/ leopard/ hyena/ lion _____

oceanographer/ biologist/ zoologist/ engineer _____

Nairobi/ Europe/ Asia/ Africa _____

9. Write a description for each reference book below.

thesaurus _____

dictionary _____

encyclopedia _____

atlas _____

almanac _____

10. List three purposes authors may use when writing.

1) _____ 2) _____ 3) _____

11. A _____ is information supported by truth, observation or science.

An _____ is a person's personal belief or thought.

Glossary

Analogy: A comparison showing how two things relate to each other. Example: **Nose is to smell as tongue is to taste** (nose : smell :: tongue : taste).

Author's Purpose: The reason why an author writes a particular story or book.

Cause: The reason something happens.

Classifying: Placing similar things into categories.

Combining Form: A word or word base used in forming words. Example: **tele** in **telephone**.

Comprehension: Understanding what is seen, read or heard.

Connotation: The meaning of a word including all the emotions associated with it.

Denotation: The literal or dictionary definition of a word.

Effect: What happens as a result of the cause.

Fact: Information that can be proven true. Example: Hawaii is a state.

Generalization: A statement or rule that applies to many situations or examples.

Homographs: Words that have the same spelling but different meanings.

Idiom: A phrase that says one thing but actually means something quite different.

Main Idea: The most important idea, or main points, in a sentence, paragraph or story.

Metaphor: A figure of speech that directly compares one thing with another. Example: **The grass is a velvet carpet**.

Opinion: Information that tells how someone feels or what he/she thinks about something. It cannot be proven.

Outline: A skeletal description of the main ideas and important details of a reading selection.

Paraphrase: To restate something in your own words.

Personification: Giving human characteristics to objects or animals.

Prefix: A syllable at the beginning of a word that changes its meaning.

Scan: To look for certain words in a reading selection to locate facts or answer questions.

Sequencing: Placing items or events in logical order.

Simile: A figure of speech comparing two things, using the words **like** or **as**. Example: **She was as quiet as a mouse**.

Skim: To read quickly to get a general idea of what a reading selection is about.

Suffix: A syllable at the end of a word that changes its meaning.

Summary: A brief retelling of the main ideas in a reading selection.

Symbolism: The use of something to stand for (symbolize) something else.

Venn Diagram: A diagram for charting information that shows similarities and differences between two things.

Answer Key

Vocabulary Building: Prefixes

A **prefix** is a syllable at the beginning of a word that changes its meaning.

Directions: Add the prefixes to the root words to make new words. The first one has been done for you.

PREFIX	MEANING	ROOT WORD	NEW WORD
pre	(before)	caution	precaution
		historic	prehistoric
mid	(middle)	night	midnight
		stream	midstream
post	(after)	graduate	postgraduate
		war	postwar

Directions: Using the meanings in parentheses, complete each sentence with one of the words you formed above. The first one has been done for you.

1. The dog howled at the moon at __midnight__. (middle of the night, 12 o'clock)

2. You must take every __precaution__ when working with chemicals. (care taken in advance)

3. She plans to do __postgraduate__ work in medicine. (a course of study after graduation)

4. The dinosaur was the biggest __prehistoric__ animal. (the time before recorded history)

5. While wading, he lost his shoe __midstream__. (in the middle of a stream)

6. The country made great progress during the early __postwar__ years. (after a war)

3

Vocabulary Building: Prefixes

Directions: Read the meanings of the following prefixes. Use each word in the box to complete the sentences. Then write another sentence using the word.

PREFIX	re	un	dis
MEANING	(again)	(not)	(apart, away)

regain	retract	undesirable	disclose
undisciplined	discontinue	unexpected	disillusion

1. She was able to __regain__ her composure after the accident.

Sentences will vary.

2. I'm afraid we'll have to __discontinue__ that line of products due to low sales.

3. She was surprised by her cousin's __unexpected__ visit.

4. He was bound by law to never __disclose__ top secret information.

5. The __undisciplined__ children ran around the grocery store knocking cans off the shelves.

6. The newspaper decided to __retract__ the damaging statements printed about the senator.

7. Those apples look completely __undesirable__ with all those bruises.

8. "I don't want to __disillusion__ you," he told her, "but the job isn't quite what you thought it would be."

4

Vocabulary Building: Prefixes

Directions: Read the meanings of the following prefixes. Add a prefix to each word in the box to make a new word that makes sense in each sentence. Use the meanings in parentheses to help.

PREFIX	MEANING
extra	beyond
inter	between
sub	below
super	above, outside
trans	across, over

marine	plant	ordinary	natural	zero	national

1. We're planning to __transplant__ the lilac bush from our front yard into our back yard. (move from one place and plant in another)

2. The book was translated and became an __international__ bestseller. (between or among nations)

3. Few animals can survive the __subzero__ temperatures in Antarctica. (below zero)

4. The __submarine__ dove deep to avoid enemy fire. (sailing vessel that can operate beneath the water)

5. He made an __extraordinary__ effort to win the race. (beyond the ordinary)

6. The empty chair moved, apparently guided by some __supernatural__ force. (occurring outside the known forces of nature)

5

Vocabulary Building: Combining Forms

A **combining form** is a word or word base used in forming words, such as **tele** in **telephone**.

Directions: Read the meanings of the combining forms. After each sentence, write the meaning for the bold word. Use a dictionary if needed. The first one has been done for you.

FORM	MEANING
uni	one, single
bi	two
tri	three
quad	four
octo	eight
dec	ten
centi	hundred

1. Do you believe the **unicorn** ever truly existed?
   a mythical animal with one horn

2. It took a **decade** for the oak tree to grow as tall as our house.
   ten years

3. On our math test, we had to find the area of a **quadrangle**.
   four-sided figure

4. The **centipede** scurried under the refrigerator when the kitchen light was turned on.
   animal with 100 legs

5. The three streets come together to form a **triangle** around our farm.
   three-sided figure

6. An **octopus** is a most unusual looking animal!
   eight-legged animal

6

Vocabulary Building: Combining Forms

Directions: Circle the combining form in each word, then use the word in a sentence.

FORM	MEANING
auto	self or self-propelled
micro	very small
petr or petro	rock or stone
tele	operating at a distance

Automatic: _____

Automobile: _____

Automotive: _____

Microphone: _____

Microscope: _____

Answers will vary.

Petrify: _____

Petroleum: _____

Telegram: _____

Telescope: _____

Television: _____

7

Vocabulary Building: Suffixes "ance" and "ous"

A **suffix** is a syllable at the end of a word that changes its meaning. Suffixes are often used to change a word to a different part of speech, such as from a verb to a noun or a noun to an adjective. The suffix **ance** means "the condition or state of being"; **ous** means "characterized by."

Directions: Add one of the suffixes to the word in parentheses to form a new word that makes sense in the sentence. The first one has been done for you.

1. Mary was very (nerve) __nervous__ the night before she starred in the class play.

2. The foolish young man spent all of his (inherit) __inheritance__ on a car.

3. The girl's (resemble) __resemblance__ to her mother is amazing.

4. A (mystery) __mysterious__ woman in black entered the room but said nothing.

5. Tonight is the final (perform) __performance__ of the opera.

6. Jimmy told the most (outrage) __outrageous__ story about why he didn't have his homework.

7. The Grand Canyon is a (marvel) __marvelous__ sight.

8. The marriage of Joyce and Ted was a (joy) __joyous__ occasion.

9. I am going to use my (allow) __allowance__ to buy a Mother's Day gift.

10. The American colonists were very (courage) __courageous__ people.

8

Vocabulary Building: Suffixes "an," "ian," "ship"

The suffixes **an** and **ian** mean "belonging to or living in," and the suffix **ship** means "the quality of or having the office of."

Directions: Combine the suffix and the root word to form a new word.

ROOT WORD	SUFFIX	NEW WORD	ROOT WORD	SUFFIX	NEW WORD
magic	ian	magician	music	ian	musician
America	an	American	Europe	an	European
friend	ship	friendship	leader	ship	leadership

Directions: Use the words you formed to complete the sentences. Then write another sentence using the word.

1. Many **European** settlers came to America to escape persecution in their home countries.

   Sentences will vary.

2. The **magician** drew gasps from the audience as he began to saw the woman in half.

3. Dr. Mathews hopes that his new position on the school board will help him to assume a **leadership** role in the community.

4. Over the many years they knew each other, their **friendship** remained strong.

5. After years of practicing the piano daily, she has become a fine **musician**

6. All **American** citizens should exercise their right to vote.

9

Vocabulary Building: "ment," "tion," "ence"

Directions: Add the suffixes **ment, tion** or **ence** to the words in the box. Then complete the sentences using the new words.

govern	connect	locate	excite
entertain	exist	correspond	concoct

1. The yearly fair created much **excitement** in the small town.

2. She could not even imagine the **concoction** being created in the kitchen.

3. Someday, she decided, she would get into politics and work for the **government** .

4. The **entertainment** for the evening included dancing, singing and a swing band.

5. I had fallen so far behind in my **correspondence** , I hadn't written a letter for months.

6. It seemed like a lonely **existence** , but she insisted she loved living alone in the mountains.

7. The telephone **connection** was severed as the construction people worked on the road.

8. That is the perfect **location** for that restaurant, for there is no other Italian food within miles.

10

Vocabulary Building: Suffixes "ism" and "ist"

The suffix **ism** means "the condition of being" or "having the characteristics of." The suffix **ist** means "one who does or is skilled at something."

Directions: Combine the suffix and root word to form a new word. Use the new word in a sentence.

1. national + ism: **nationalism**

2. patriot + ism: **patriotism**

   Sentences will vary.

3. alcohol + ism: **alcoholism**

4. criticize + ism: **criticism**

5. archaeology + ist: **archaeologist**

6. violin + ist: **violinist**

7. terror + ist: **terrorist**

8. chemistry + ist: **chemist**

9. piano + ist: **pianist**

11

Review

Directions: Add one of the prefixes, suffixes or combining forms to a word in the box to complete each sentence. Use the definition in parentheses as a clue.

ian	ous	ship	an	ist	extra	trans	pre	micro	super

friend	music	geology	sensory	America
paid	wave	market	atlantic	danger

1. The **supermarket** has a huge selection of fruits and vegetables. (large food store)

2. The first **transatlantic** flight was a remarkable feat in the history of aviation. (across the Atlantic Ocean)

3. The woman claimed that she knew the future because of her **extrasensory** capabilities. (beyond the normal senses)

4. When mailing your payment, please use the **prepaid** envelope. (paid in advance)

5. Mrs. Johnson studied the violin for many years to become the accomplished **musician** she is today. (person skilled in music)

6. The **microwave** oven is a modern-day convenience. (operating with extremely small electromagnetic waves)

7. Lightning is the most **dangerous** part of a storm. (characterized by danger)

8. They raised the **American** flag over their campground in a gesture of patriotism. (belonging to America)

9. The Native Americans would often smoke a peace pipe as a sign of **friendship** . (the state of being friends)

10. Dr. Stokes is the finest **geologist** at the university. (one who is skilled in geology, the study of the earth's crust)

12

Review

Directions: Add one of the following prefixes or suffixes to the words in the box to complete each sentence. Use the definition in parentheses as a clue.

tion	al	ment	ence	re	un	dis

establish	place	estimate
courage	persist	acceptable

1. He will **replace** the broken vase next week. (take the place of)

2. I will not **discourage** you from traveling to Europe. (not persuade)

3. The restaurant on the corner is the newest eating **establishment** in the city. (business)

4. Your **estimation** of the amount of money in the jar is surprisingly accurate. (appraisal)

5. Her poor work is **unacceptable** . (not allowable)

6. His **persistence** paid off when he graduated with his doctoral degree. (steadfast effort)

Directions: Write at least two words for each of the following suffixes, then write a sentence for each.

ism _____

Answers will vary.

ish _____

13

Vocabulary Building: Homographs

A **homograph** has the same spelling as another word but a different meaning. The two words are often different parts of speech.

Directions: Write the definition from the box for the bold word in each sentence.

con' tract	n.	an agreement to do something
con tract'	v.	to reduce in size, shrink
des' ert	n.	dry land that can support little plant and animal life
de sert'	v.	to abandon
Po' lish	adj.	of or belonging to Poland
pol' ish	v.	to smooth and brighten by rubbing
proj' ect	n.	a proposal or undertaking
pro ject'	v.	to send forth in thoughts or imagination

1. Iron is one of the metals that **contracts** as it cools.
   to reduce in size, shrink

2. You will have to sign a **contract** before I can begin work on your house.
   an agreement to do something

3. The **desert** seems to come to life in the evening when the animals come out in search of food.
   dry land that can support little plant and animal life

4. I hope you will not **desert** your friends now that they really need your support.
   to abandon

5. She will **polish** the stone and then use it to make a necklace.
   to smooth and brighten by rubbing

6. The **Polish** people have been courageous in their struggle for freedom.
   of or belonging to Poland

7. **Project** yourself into the world of tomorrow with this amazing invention!
   to send forth in thoughts or imagination

8. I started this **project** on Monday, but it may be weeks before I finish it.
   a proposal or undertaking

14

Vocabulary Building: Homographs

Directions: After each sentence, write the meaning of the bold word. Write another sentence using a homograph for the word.

1. The owner of the pet store tied a bright red **bow** around the puppies' necks.
Meaning: <u>a knot tied with a ribbon</u>
Sentence:

2. Today, fewer pipes are made from **lead**.
Meaning: <u>a metal</u>
Sentence:

3. Marcia's new house is very **close** to ours.
Meaning: <u>near</u>
Sentence:

4. Please **record** the time and day that we finished the project.
Meaning: <u>write down</u>
Sentence:

5. It takes only a **minute** to fasten your seatbelt, but it can save your life.
Meaning: <u>60 seconds</u>
Sentence:

6. I cannot **subject** the animal to that kind of treatment.
Meaning: <u>expose</u>
Sentence:

> Sentences will vary.

15

Vocabulary Building: Multiple Meanings

Directions: Use a dictionary to choose the correct definition for each bold word. The first one has been done for you.

1. My grandfather always has his **spectacles** perched on his nose.
Meaning: <u>lenses worn in front of the eyes to aid vision</u>

2. The Fourth of July fireworks display was an amazing **spectacle**.
Meaning: <u>dramatic public display</u>

3. We enjoy a rugged vacation, staying in a hunting **lodge** rather than a hotel.
Meaning: <u>large rustic cabin for vacationers</u>

4. Don't let the baby have hard candy, because it could **lodge** in his throat.
Meaning: <u>get stuck</u>

5. Termites will **bore** through the rotten wood in our basement if we don't have it replaced.
Meaning: <u>to make a hole by digging</u>

6. That television show could **bore** even a small child!
Meaning: <u>to weary by being dull</u>

7. Don't **resort** to lies just to get what you want!
Meaning: <u>to go back to habitually</u>

8. The **resort** is packed with tourists from May to September each year.
Meaning: <u>place providing recreation and entertainment</u>

16

Vocabulary Building: Multiple Meanings

Directions: Read each sentence, then write another sentence using a different meaning for the bold word.

1. The prince will **succeed** his mother as ruler of the country.

2. All through the National Anthem, Johnny was singing in the wrong **key**.

3. There has been only a **trace** of rain this month.

4. I can't get involved in a **cause** in which I don't really believe.

5. It is very impor

6. A police officer can **issue** a warning to those disturbing the peace.

7. There is a mayoral candidate from each of the major political **parties**.

8. You can take that **stack** of newspapers to be recycled.

9. The judge will likely **sentence** the offender to a year in prison.

10. The lawyer made a **motion** to have the charges dropped.

> Answers will vary.

17

Vocabulary Building: Similes

A **simile** is a figure of speech comparing two things using **like** or **as**.
Example: The child was as quiet as a mouse.
Directions: Read the following paragraph. Underline the similes.

The kittens were born on a morning <u>as cold as ice</u>. Although it was late spring, the weather hadn't quite warmed up. There were five kittens in the litter, each quite different from its siblings. The oldest was <u>black as deepest night</u>. There was a calico that looked <u>like Grandma's old quilt</u>. One was <u>as orange as a fall pumpkin</u>, and another was orange and white. The runt was a black and gray tiger. She was <u>as little as a baseball</u> and <u>as quick as lightning</u> to fight for food. The kittens will soon become accepted by the other animals as members of the farm.

Directions: Using the following words, create similes of your own.
Example: piano—The piano keys tinkled like a light rain on a tin roof.

> Sample answers:

1. fire <u>The fire was as hot as a furnace.</u>

2. thunderstorm <u>The thunderstorm was like an angry old man.</u>

3. ocean <u>The ocean was as blue as the sky.</u>

4. night <u>The night was as black as pitch.</u>

5. rainforest <u>The rainforest was like a breath of fresh air.</u>

6. giraffe <u>The giraffe is as tall as our house!</u>

18

Vocabulary Building: Metaphors

A **metaphor** is a figure of speech that directly compares one thing with another.
Example: As it set, the sun was a glowing orange ball of fire.
The sun is being compared to a glowing orange ball of fire.
<u>sun</u>   <u>glowing orange ball of fire</u>
Directions: Underline the metaphor in each sentence. Then write the two things that are being compared on the lines.

1. The ocean, a swirling mass of anger, released its fury on the shore.
<u>ocean</u>   <u>swirling mass of anger</u>

2. He was a top spinning out of control.
<u>He</u>   <u>top spinning out of control</u>

3. The heat covered the crowd, a blanket smothering them all.
<u>heat</u>   <u>blanket smothering them all</u>

4. I fed my dog a steak, and it was a banquet for her senses.
<u>steak</u>   <u>banquet for her senses</u>

5. The flowers in the garden were a stained glass window.
<u>flowers</u>   <u>stained glass window</u>

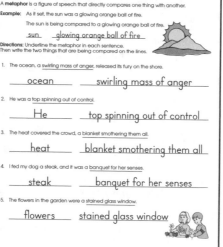

19

Vocabulary Building: Metaphors and Similes

Directions: Underline the metaphors in the following sentences. Then rewrite each sentence using a simile.

1. She is a playful child, a real <u>kitten</u>!
<u>She is as playful as a kitten.</u>

2. Life today is a <u>merry-go-round</u>.
<u>Life is like a merry-go-round.</u>

3. His emotions were <u>waves washing over him</u>.
<u>His emotions were like waves washing over him.</u>

4. His childhood was an <u>image in a rearview mirror</u>.
<u>His childhood was like an image in a rearview mirror.</u>

Directions: Write the meanings of the following sentences.

> Sample answers:

1. His mind was as changeable as spring weather.
<u>His mind was likely to change all the time.</u>

2. His demand was like a clap of thunder.
<u>His demand was loud and scary.</u>

3. There was joy written on the children's faces on Christmas morning.
<u>The children's faces had joyful expressions.</u>

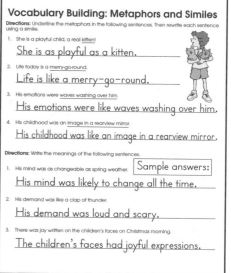

20

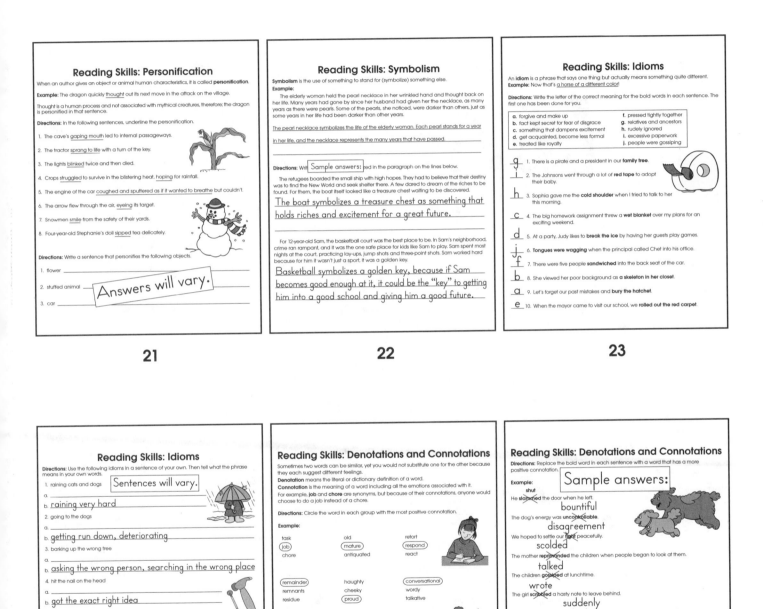

Reading Skills: Personification

When an author gives an object or animal human characteristics, it is called **personification**.

Example: The dragon quickly thought out its next move in the attack on the village.

Thought is a human process and not associated with mythical creatures, therefore; the dragon is personified in that sentence.

Directions: In the following sentences, underline the personification.

1. The cave's gaping mouth led to internal passageways.

2. The tractor sprang to life with a turn of the key.

3. The lights blinked twice and then died.

4. Crops struggled to survive in the blistering heat, hoping for rainfall.

5. The engine of the car coughed and sputtered as if it wanted to breathe but couldn't.

6. The arrow flew through the air, eyeing its target.

7. Snowmen smile from the safety of their yards.

8. Four-year-old Stephanie's doll sipped tea delicately.

Directions: Write a sentence that personifies the following objects.

1. flower _____

2. stuffed animal   Answers will vary.

3. car _____

21

Reading Skills: Symbolism

Symbolism is the use of something to stand for (symbolize) something else.
Example:

The elderly woman held the pearl necklace in her wrinkled hand and thought back on her life. Many years had gone by since her husband had given her the necklace, as many years as there were pearls. Some of the pearls, she noticed, were darker than others, just as some years in her life had been darker than other years.

The pearl necklace symbolizes the life of the elderly woman. Each pearl stands for a year in her life, and the necklace represents the many years that have passed.

Directions: Write [Sample answers:]zed in the paragraph on the lines below.

The refugees boarded the small ship with high hopes. They had to believe that their destiny was to find the New World and seek shelter there. A few dared to dream of the riches to be found. For them, the boat itself looked like a treasure chest waiting to be discovered.

The boat symbolizes a treasure chest as something that holds riches and excitement for a great future.

For 12-year-old Sam, the basketball court was the best place to be. In Sam's neighborhood, crime ran rampant, and it was the one safe place for kids like Sam to play. Sam spent most nights at the court, practicing lay-ups, jump shots and three-point shots. Sam worked hard because for him it wasn't just a sport, it was a golden key.

Basketball symbolizes a golden key, because if Sam becomes good enough at it, it could be the "key" to getting him into a good school and giving him a good future.

22

Reading Skills: Idioms

An **idiom** is a phrase that says one thing but actually means something quite different.
Example: Now that's a horse of a different color!

Directions: Write the letter of the correct meaning for the bold words in each sentence. The first one has been done for you.

a. forgive and make up
b. fact kept secret for fear of disgrace
c. something that dampens excitement
d. get acquainted, become less formal
e. treated like royalty
f. pressed tightly together
g. relatives and ancestors
h. rudely ignored
i. excessive paperwork
j. people were gossiping

g 1. There is a pirate and a president in our **family tree**.

i 2. The Johnsons went through a lot of **red tape** to adopt their baby.

h 3. Sophia gave me the **cold shoulder** when I tried to talk to her this morning.

c 4. The big homework assignment threw a **wet blanket** over my plans for an exciting weekend.

d 5. At a party, Judy likes to **break the ice** by having her guests play games.

j 6. **Tongues were wagging** when the principal called Chet into his office.

f 7. There were five people **sandwiched** into the back seat of the car.

b 8. She viewed her poor background as a **skeleton in her closet**.

a 9. Let's forget our past mistakes and **bury the hatchet**.

e 10. When the mayor came to visit our school, we **rolled out the red carpet**.

23

Reading Skills: Idioms

Directions: Use the following idioms in a sentence of your own. Then tell what the phrase means in your own words.   Sentences will vary.

1. raining cats and dogs
a. _____
b. raining very hard

2. going to the dogs
a. _____
b. getting run down, deteriorating

3. barking up the wrong tree
a. _____
b. asking the wrong person, searching in the wrong place

4. hit the nail on the head
a. _____
b. got the exact right idea

5. went out on a limb
a. _____
b. took a chance

6. all in the same boat
a. _____
b. all in the same situation

7. keep up with the Joneses
a. _____
b. keep up with the people around you

24

Reading Skills: Denotations and Connotations

Sometimes two words can be similar, yet you would not substitute one for the other because they each suggest different feelings.
Denotation means the literal or dictionary definition of a word.
Connotation is the meaning of a word including all the emotions associated with it.
For example, **job** and **chore** are synonyms, but because of their connotations, anyone would choose to do a job instead of a chore.

Directions: Circle the word in each group with the most positive connotation.

Example:

task	old	retort
(job)	(mature)	(respond)
chore	antiquated	react

(remainder)	haughty	(conversational)
remnants	cheeky	wordy
residue	(proud)	talkative

excessively	(relaxed)	shack
grossly	lazy	hovel
(abundantly)	inactive	(hut)

curious	(swift)	(scamp)
prying	hasty	rascal
nosy	speedy	hoodlum

25

Reading Skills: Denotations and Connotations

Directions: Replace the bold word in each sentence with a word that has a more positive connotation.

Example: Sample answers:
shut
He slammed the door when he left.

bountiful
The dog's energy was uncontrollable.

disagreement
We hoped to settle our fight peacefully.

scolded
The mother reprimanded the children when people began to look at them.

talked
The children gossiped at lunchtime.

wrote
The girl scribbled a hasty note to leave behind.

suddenly
Our conversation ended abruptly when the phone rang.

serious
The principal was a severe man.

took
The boy snatched the toy from his baby brother.

refused
The couple rejected their offer of help.

messy
Dad reminded me to clean my disastrous room.

26

Reading Skills: Denotations and Connotations

Directions: The words in each group have a similar denotation, but one word has a connotation that suggests a negative feeling or idea. Circle the word with the negative connotation. The first one has been done for you.

1. (stun)
   amaze
   astound

2. embarrassed
   (ashamed)
   blushing

3. chat
   discuss
   (gossip)

4. mischievous
   playful
   (unruly)

5. dirty
   (filthy)
   soiled

6. small
   (puny)
   miniature

7. (abandon)
   leave
   depart

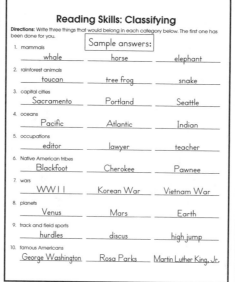

Directions: Write the word with the best connotation to complete each sentence.

1. Because he has had the flu for a few days, Mike's face looks very ___pale___ .
   (ghostly, pale, bloodless)

2. We will have to ___reduce___ the amount of food we waste.
   (lower, shrink, reduce)

3. Did you get a good ___recommendation___ from your former employer?
   (reference, mention, recommendation)

4. There was an ___outbreak___ of measles at our school.
   (attack, occurrence, outbreak)

27

Review

Directions: Circle the word or phrase that best defines the bold words in each sentence.

1. What is the **subject** of the report you are writing for class?
   to cause to undergo
   (topic)
   course of study

2. Will you be going to the same **resort** where you spent your vacation last year?
   turn to for use or help
   to sort again
   (place for rest and relaxation)

3. They **rolled out the red carpet** for the contest winners.
   unrolled carpeting
   (treated like royalty)
   showed appreciation for

4. Mitch's past as a prisoner was **a skeleton in his closet.**
   (fact kept secret for fear of disgrace)
   dead person
   ancestor

5. Sally decided to **bury the hatchet** and called her sister to apologize.
   say she was sorry
   (forget past mistakes and make up)
   go hunting

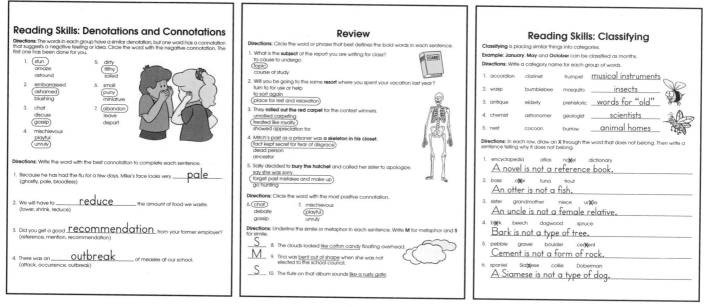

Directions: Circle the word with the most positive connotation.

6. (chat)
   debate
   gossip

7. mischievous
   (playful)
   unruly

Directions: Underline the simile or metaphor in each sentence. Write **M** for metaphor and **S** for simile.

S 8. The clouds looked <u>like cotton candy</u> floating overhead.

M 9. Tina was <u>bent out of shape</u> when she was not elected to the school council.

S 10. The flute on that album sounds <u>like a rusty gate.</u>

28

Reading Skills: Classifying

Classifying is placing similar things into categories.

Example: January, May and October can be classified as months.

Directions: Write a category name for each group of words.

1. accordion   clarinet   trumpet   ___musical instruments___

2. wasp   bumblebee   mosquito   ___insects___

3. antique   elderly   prehistoric   ___words for "old"___

4. chemist   astronomer   geologist   ___scientists___

5. nest   cocoon   burrow   ___animal homes___

Directions: In each row, draw an **X** through the word that does not belong. Then write a sentence telling why it does not belong.

1. encyclopedia   atlas   ~~novel~~   dictionary
   A novel is not a reference book.

2. bass   ~~otter~~   tuna   trout
   An otter is not a fish.

3. sister   grandmother   niece   ~~uncle~~
   An uncle is not a female relative.

4. ~~bark~~   beech   dogwood   spruce
   Bark is not a type of tree.

5. pebble   gravel   boulder   ~~cement~~
   Cement is not a form of rock.

6. spaniel   ~~Siamese~~   collie   Doberman
   A Siamese is not a type of dog.

29

Reading Skills: Classifying

Directions: In each row, draw an **X** through the word that does not belong. Then write a word that belongs.

Sample answers:

1. monkey   ~~elephant~~   ~~grizzly~~~~bear~~   ___giraffe___

2. daisies   roses   violets   ~~ferns~~   pansies   ___tulips___

3. paper   ~~pin~~   pencil   eraser   stapler   ___pen___

4. sister   cousin   father   aunt   ~~friend~~   ___mother___

5. hand   mouth   ~~shirt~~   foot   elbow   ___leg___

6. shy   ~~ox~~   happy   angry   sad   ___grumpy___

7. puppy   ~~dog~~   kitten   cub   lamb   ___chick___

8. red   blue   ~~color~~   yellow   purple   ___green___

9. Earth   Jupiter   Saturn   Pluto   ~~Sun~~   ___Mars___

10. ~~sink~~   bed   desk   dresser   lamp   ___chair___

Directions: Name each category above.

1. ___African animals___

2. ___flowers___

3. ___school supplies___

4. ___relatives___

5. ___body parts___

6. ___feelings___

7. ___baby animals___

8. ___colors___

9. ___planets___

10. ___bedroom furniture___

30

Reading Skills: Classifying

Directions: Write three things that would belong in each category below. The first one has been done for you.

1. mammals
   Sample answers:
   ___whale___   ___horse___   ___elephant___

2. rainforest animals
   ___toucan___   ___tree frog___   ___snake___

3. capital cities
   ___Sacramento___   ___Portland___   ___Seattle___

4. oceans
   ___Pacific___   ___Atlantic___   ___Indian___

5. occupations
   ___editor___   ___lawyer___   ___teacher___

6. Native American tribes
   ___Blackfoot___   ___Cherokee___   ___Pawnee___

7. wars
   ___WWII___   ___Korean War___   ___Vietnam War___

8. planets
   ___Venus___   ___Mars___   ___Earth___

9. track and field sports
   ___hurdles___   ___discus___   ___high jump___

10. famous Americans
    ___George Washington___   ___Rosa Parks___   ___Martin Luther King, Jr.___

31

Reading Skills: Analogies

An **analogy** is a comparison showing how two things relate to each other. Analogies can show part/whole relationships, antonyms (words with opposite meanings), synonyms (words with the same meaning) and cause/effect relationships. When reading an analogy, say, "Hot is to cold as day is to night." When writing an analogy, use colons.

Example: hot : cold :: day : night

Directions: Complete each analogy using a word from the box.

| seize | vault | sleep | cooperative | rich |

1. ambush : trap :: catch : ___seize___

2. communicate : tell :: crypt : ___vault___

3. unscrupulous : dishonorable :: docile : ___cooperative___

4. edible : digestible :: rest : ___sleep___

5. mischievous : frolicsome :: wealthy : ___rich___

| enhance | private | careless | permit | illogical |

6. minority : majority :: public : ___private___

7. painstaking : haphazard :: selective : ___careless___

8. reduce : increase :: diminish : ___enhance___

9. refuse : consent :: deny : ___permit___

10. sane : insane :: logical : ___illogical___

32

Reading Skills: Analogies

Directions: Complete each analogy using a word from the box. The first one has been done for you.

| positive | wires | flower | tape | descend | drink | commercial |
| grape | house | mouth | rude | bill | melted | worker | four |

1. banana : peel :: walnut : _____shell_____
2. bird : beak :: duck : _____bill_____
3. up : ascend :: down : _____descend_____
4. cathedral : church :: mansion : _____house_____
5. discourage : encourage :: negative : _____positive_____
6. nasal : nose :: oral : _____mouth_____
7. prune : plum :: raisin : _____grape_____
8. hunger : eat :: thirst : _____drink_____
9. icicle : frozen :: water : _____melted_____
10. dandelion : weed :: lilac : _____flower_____
11. polite : impolite :: courteous : _____rude_____
12. plumber : pipes :: electrician : _____wires_____
13. employer : employee :: boss : _____worker_____
14. camera : film :: VCR : _____tape_____
15. triangle : three :: square : _____four_____
16. newspaper : advertisement :: television : _____commercial_____

33

Reading Skills: Analogies

Directions: Complete each analogy using a word from the box. Write the analogy as a sentence. The first one has been done for you.

| engine | herd | frog | soft | White House | wings | boat | garage |

1. red : stop :: yellow : _____caution_____
Red is to stop as yellow is to caution.

2. bird : flock :: cattle : _____herd_____
Bird is to flock as cattle is to herd.

3. caterpillar : butterfly :: tadpole : _____frog_____
Caterpillar is to butterfly as tadpole is to frog.

4. queen : palace :: United States president : _____White House_____
Queen is to palace as United States president is to White House.

5. automobile : wheels :: airplane : _____wings_____
Automobile is to wheels as airplane is to wings.

6. astronaut : spacecraft :: sailor : _____boat_____
Astronaut is to spacecraft as sailor is to boat.

7. sailboat : wind :: airplane : _____engine_____
Sailboat is to wind as airplane is to engine.

8. stone : hard :: grass : _____soft_____
Stone is to hard as grass is to soft.

9. airplane : hangar :: automobile : _____garage_____
Airplane is to hangar as automobile is to garage.

34

Reading Skills: Fact or Opinion?

A **fact** is information that can be proved. An **opinion** is information that tells how someone feels or what he/she thinks about something.

Directions: For each sentence, write **F** for fact or **O** for opinion. The first one has been done for you.

__F__ 1. Each of the countries in South America has its own capital.
__O__ 2. All South Americans are good swimmers.
__O__ 3. People like the climate in Peru better than in Brazil.
__F__ 4. The continent of South America is almost completely surrounded by water.
__F__ 5. The only connection with another continent is a narrow strip of land, called the Isthmus of Panama, which links it to North America.
__F__ 6. The Andes Mountains run all the way down the western edge of the continent.
__F__ 7. The Andes is the longest continuous mountain barrier in the world.
__O__ 8. The Andes are the most beautiful mountain range.
__F__ 9. The Amazon River is the second longest river in the world—about 4,000 miles long.
__F__ 10. Half of the people in South America are Brazilians.
__O__ 11. Life in Brazil is better than life in other South American countries.
__O__ 12. Brazil is the best place for South Americans to live.
__F__ 13. Cape Horn is at the southern tip of South America.
__F__ 14. The largest land animal in South America is the tapir, which reaches a length of 6 to 8 feet.

35

Reading Skills: Fact or Opinion?

Directions: Read the paragraphs below. For each numbered sentence, write **F** for fact or **O** for opinion. Write the reason for your answer. The first one has been done for you.

(1) The two greatest poems in the history of the world are the *Iliad* and the *Odyssey*. (2) The *Iliad* is the story of the Trojan War; the *Odyssey* tells about the wanderings of the Greek hero Ulysses after the war. (3) These poems are so long that they each fill an entire book.

(4) The author of the poems, according to Greek legend, was a blind poet named Homer. (5) Almost nothing is known about Homer. (6) This indicates to me that it is possible that Homer never existed. (7) Maybe Homer existed but didn't write the *Iliad* and the *Odyssey*.

(8) Whether or not there was a Homer does not really matter. We have these wonderful poems, w~~ritten more~~ than 2,500 years after they were written.

Sample answers:

1. __O__ Reason: This cannot be proven. People have different opinions about which are the greatest poems.
2. __F__ Reason: explains what the poems are about
3. __F__ Reason: tells how long the poems are
4. __F__ Reason: tells a fact about a Greek legend
5. __F__ Reason: tells that not much is known about Homer
6. __O__ Reason: not everyone thinks Homer did not exist
7. __O__ Reason: some people may believe this and some may not
8. __O__ Reason: some people may not agree with this

36

Reading Skills: It's Your Opinion

Your opinion is how you feel or think about something. Although other people may have the same opinion, their reasons could not be exactly the same because of their individuality.

When writing an opinion paragraph, it is important to first state your opinion. Then, in at least three sentences, support your opinion. Finally, end your paragraph by restating your opinion in different words.

Example:
I believe dogs are excellent pets. For thousands of years, dogs have guarded and protected their owners. Dogs are faithful and have been known to save the lives of those they love. Dogs offer unconditional love as well as company for the quiet times in our lives. For these reasons, I feel that dogs make wonderful pets.

Directions: Write an opinion paragraph on whether you would or would not like to have lived in Colonial America. Be sure to support your opinion with at least three reasons.

Answers will vary.

Writing Checklist

Reread your paragraph carefully.
- [ ] My paragraph makes sense.
- [ ] There are no jumps in ideas.
- [ ] I used correct punctuation.
- [ ] I have a good opening and ending.
- [ ] I used correct spelling.
- [ ] My paragraph is well-organized.
- [ ] My paragraph is interesting.

37

Reading Skills: Cause and Effect

A **cause** is the reason something happens. The **effect** is what happens as the result of the cause.

Directions: Read the paragraphs below. For each numbered sentence, circle the cause or causes and underline the effect or effects. The first one has been done for you.

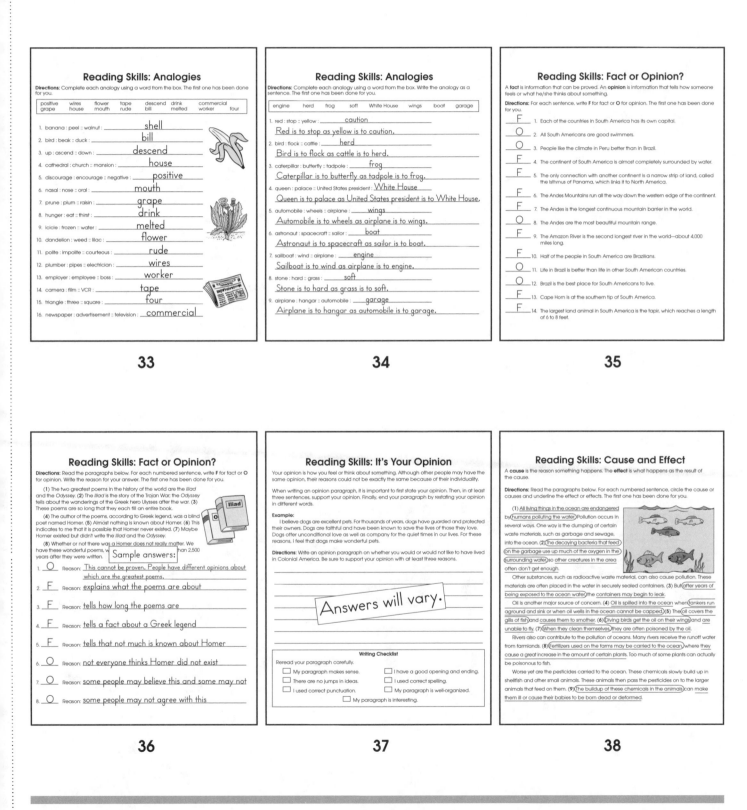

(1) All living things in the ocean are endangered by humans polluting the water. Pollution occurs in several ways. One way is the dumping of certain waste materials, such as garbage and sewage, into the ocean. (2) The decaying bacteria that feed on the garbage use up much of the oxygen in the surrounding water, so other creatures in the area often don't get enough.

Other substances, such as radioactive waste material, can also cause pollution. These materials are often placed in the water in securely sealed containers. (3) But after years of being exposed to the ocean water, the containers may begin to leak.

Oil is another major source of concern. (4) Oil is spilled into the ocean when tankers run aground and sink or when oil wells in the ocean cannot be capped. (5) The oil covers the gills of fish and causes them to smother. (6) Diving birds get the oil on their wings and are unable to fly. (7) When they clean themselves, they are often poisoned by the oil.

Rivers also can contribute to the pollution of oceans. Many rivers receive the runoff water from farmlands. (8) Fertilizers used on the farms may be carried to the ocean, where they cause a great increase in the amount of certain plants. Too much of some plants can actually be poisonous to fish.

Worse yet are the pesticides carried to the ocean. These chemicals slowly build up in shellfish and other small animals. These animals then pass the pesticides on to the larger animals that feed on them. (9) The buildup of these chemicals in the animals can make them ill or cause their babies to be born dead or deformed.

38

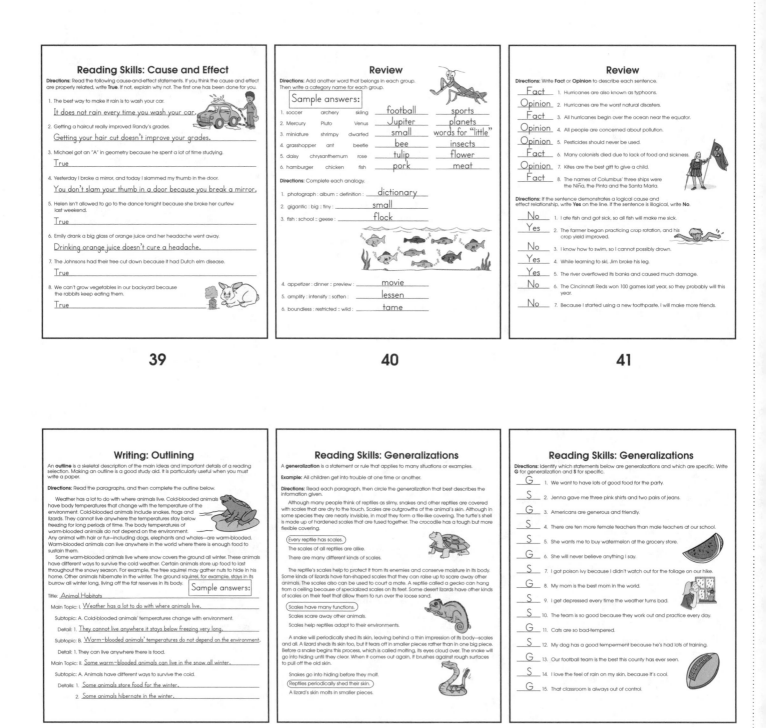

Reading Skills: Cause and Effect

Directions: Read the following cause-and-effect statements. If you think the cause and effect are properly related, write **True**. If not, explain why not. The first one has been done for you.

1. The best way to make it rain is to wash your car.
It does not rain every time you wash your car.

2. Getting a haircut really improved Randy's grades.
Getting your hair cut doesn't improve your grades.

3. Michael got an "A" in geometry because he spent a lot of time studying.
True

4. Yesterday I broke a mirror, and today I slammed my thumb in the door.
You don't slam your thumb in a door because you break a mirror.

5. Helen isn't allowed to go to the dance tonight because she broke her curfew last weekend.
True

6. Emily drank a big glass of orange juice and her headache went away.
Drinking orange juice doesn't cure a headache.

7. The Johnsons had their tree cut down because it had Dutch elm disease.
True

8. We can't grow vegetables in our backyard because the rabbits keep eating them.
True

39

Review

Directions: Add another word that belongs in each group. Then write a category name for each group.

Sample answers:

1. soccer	archery	skiing	football	sports
2. Mercury	Pluto	Venus	Jupiter	planets
3. miniature	shrimpy	dwarfed	small	words for "little"
4. grasshopper	ant	beetle	bee	insects
5. daisy	chrysanthemum	rose	tulip	flower
6. hamburger	chicken	fish	pork	meat

Directions: Complete each analogy.

1. photograph : album :: definition : _dictionary_
2. gigantic : big :: tiny : _small_
3. fish : school :: geese : _flock_

4. appetizer : dinner :: preview : _movie_
5. amplify : intensify :: soften : _lessen_
6. boundless : restricted :: wild : _tame_

40

Review

Directions: Write **Fact** or **Opinion** to describe each sentence.

Fact 1. Hurricanes are also known as typhoons.
Opinion 2. Hurricanes are the worst natural disasters.
Fact 3. All hurricanes begin over the ocean near the equator.
Opinion 4. All people are concerned about pollution.
Opinion 5. Pesticides should never be used.
Fact 6. Many colonists died due to lack of food and sickness.
Opinion 7. Kites are the best gift to give a child.
Fact 8. The names of Columbus' three ships were the Niña, the Pinta and the Santa Maria.

Directions: If the sentence demonstrates a logical cause and effect relationship, write **Yes** on the line. If the sentence is illogical, write **No**.

_No_ 1. I ate fish and got sick, so all fish will make me sick.
Yes 2. The farmer began practicing crop rotation, and his crop yield improved.
_No_ 3. I know how to swim, so I cannot possibly drown.
Yes 4. While learning to ski, Jim broke his leg.
Yes 5. The river overflowed its banks and caused much damage.
_No_ 6. The Cincinnati Reds won 100 games last year, so they probably will this year.
_No_ 7. Because I started using a new toothpaste, I will make more friends.

41

Writing: Outlining

An **outline** is a skeletal description of the main ideas and important details of a reading selection. Making an outline is a good study aid. It is particularly useful when you must write a paper.

Directions: Read the paragraphs, and then complete the outline below.

Weather has a lot to do with where animals live. Cold-blooded animals have body temperatures that change with the temperature of the environment. Cold-blooded animals include snakes, frogs and lizards. They cannot live anywhere the temperatures stay below freezing for long periods of time. The body temperatures of warm-blooded animals do not depend on the environment. Any animal with hair or fur—including dogs, elephants and whales—are warm-blooded. Warm-blooded animals can live anywhere in the world where there is enough food to sustain them.

Some warm-blooded animals live where snow covers the ground all winter. These animals have different ways to survive the cold weather. Certain animals store up food to last throughout the snowy season. For example, the tree squirrel may gather nuts to hide in his home. Other animals hibernate in the winter. The ground squirrel, for example, stays in its burrow all winter long, living off the fat reserves in its body.

Sample answers:

Title: _Animal Habitats_

Main Topic: I. _Weather has a lot to do with where animals live._

Subtopic: A. Cold-blooded animals' temperatures change with environment.

Detail: 1. _They cannot live anywhere it stays below freezing very long._

Subtopic: B. _Warm-blooded animals' temperatures do not depend on the environment._

Detail: 1. They can live anywhere there is food.

Main Topic: II. _Some warm-blooded animals can live in the snow all winter._

Subtopic: A. Animals have different ways to survive the cold.

Details: 1. _Some animals store food for the winter._

2. _Some animals hibernate in the winter._

42

Reading Skills: Generalizations

A **generalization** is a statement or rule that applies to many situations or examples.

Example: All children get into trouble at one time or another.

Directions: Read each paragraph, then circle the generalization that best describes the information given.

Although many people think of reptiles as slimy, snakes and other reptiles are covered with scales that are dry to the touch. Scales are outgrowths of the animal's skin. Although in some species they are nearly invisible, in most they form a tile-like covering. The turtle's shell is made up of hardened scales that are fused together. The crocodile has a tough but more flexible covering.

(Every reptile has scales.)
The scales of all reptiles are alike.
There are many different kinds of scales.

The reptile's scales help to protect it from its enemies and conserve moisture in its body. Some kinds of lizards have fan-shaped scales that they can raise up to scare away other animals. The scales also can be used to court a mate. A reptile called a gecko can hang from a ceiling because of specialized scales on its feet. Some desert lizards have other kinds of scales on their feet that allow them to run over the loose sand.

(Scales have many functions.)
Scales scare away other animals.
Scales help reptiles adapt to their environments.

A snake will periodically shed its skin, leaving behind a thin impression of its body—scales and all. A lizard sheds its skin too, but it tears off in smaller pieces rather than in one big piece. Before a snake begins this process, which is called molting, its eyes cloud over. The snake will go into hiding until they clear. When it comes out again, it brushes against rough surfaces to pull off the old skin.

Snakes go into hiding before they molt.
(Reptiles periodically shed their skin.)
A lizard's skin molts in smaller pieces.

43

Reading Skills: Generalizations

Directions: Identify which statements below are generalizations and which are specific. Write **G** for generalization and **S** for specific.

_G_ 1. We want to have lots of good food for the party.
_S_ 2. Jenna gave me three pink shirts and two pairs of jeans.
_G_ 3. Americans are generous and friendly.
_S_ 4. There are ten more female teachers than male teachers at our school.
_S_ 5. She wants me to buy watermelon at the grocery store.
_G_ 6. She will never believe anything I say.
_S_ 7. I got poison ivy because I didn't watch out for the foliage on our hike.
_G_ 8. My mom is the best mom in the world.
_S_ 9. I get depressed every time the weather turns bad.
_S_ 10. The team is so good because they work out and practice every day.
_G_ 11. Cats are so bad-tempered.
_S_ 12. My dog has a good temperament because he's had lots of training.
_G_ 13. Our football team is the best this county has ever seen.
_S_ 14. I love the feel of rain on my skin, because it's cool.
_G_ 15. That classroom is always out of control.

44

114

Writing: Summarizing

A **summary** is a brief retelling of the main ideas of a reading selection. To summarize, write the author's most important points in your own words.

Directions: Write a two-sentence summary for each paragraph.

The boll weevil is a small beetle that is native to Mexico. It feeds inside the seed pods, or bolls, of cotton plants. The boll weevil crossed into Texas in the late 1800s. It has since spread into most of the cotton-growing areas of the United States. The boll weevil causes hundreds of millions of dollars worth of damage to cotton crops each year.

Summary: _____

Each spring, fe_____ Answers will vary.
with their snouts. T_____
into wormlike grub_____ causing the buds to
fall from the plant. _____ way from one bud to another. Several
generations of boll weevils may be produced in a single season.

Summary: _____

The coming of the boll weevil to the United States caused tremendous damage to cotton crops. Yet, there were some good results, too. Farmers were forced to plant other crops. In areas where a variety of crops were raised, the land is in better condition than it would have been if only cotton had been grown.

Summary: _____

45

Writing: Summarizing a Personal Narrative

Directions: Read the following narrative, then follow the directions.

My Greatest Fear

I am scared of spiders. I realize this is not a logical fear, but I cannot help myself. I have been frightened by spiders since I was very young. For the following three reasons, spiders will never be pets of mine.

The first reason that I am scared of spiders is their appearance. I do not like their eight wispy, creepy legs. Spiders are never easily seen, but rather dark and unattractive. They are often hairy, and the mere thought of multiple eyeballs gives me shivers.

Spiders are not well-behaved. They are sly and always ready to sneak up on innocent victims. Spiders have habits of scurrying across floors, dropping from ceilings, and dangling from cobwebs. One never knows what to expect from a spider.

Finally, I am scared of spiders due to a "spider experience" as a child. Having just climbed into bed, I noticed a particularly nasty-looking spider on the ceiling over my bed. My father came into dispose of it, and it fell into bed with me. The thought of it crawling over me drove me from the bed shrieking. After that, I checked the ceiling nightly before getting into bed.

Many people love spiders. They are good for the environment and are certainly needed on our planet. However, because of my fear, irrational though it may be, I'd rather just avoid contact with arachnids.

Directions: Write a four-sentence summary of the narrative.

Answers will vary.

46

Writing: Summarizing a Personal Narrative

Write the main idea of the second paragraph.

The author doesn't like spiders because of their appearance.

Write the main idea of the third paragraph.

The author doesn't like spiders because they are not well-behaved.

Write the main idea of the fourth paragraph.

The author doesn't like spiders because of a bad experience as a child.

Everyone has a fear of something. On another sheet of paper, write a five-paragraph personal narrative about a fear of your own. Use the following guide to help you organize your narrative.

Paragraph 1. State your fear.

Provide background information about fear.

Paragraph 2. State your first reason for fear.

Support this state_____

Answers will vary.
_____ three sentences.

Paragraph 4. State your third reason for fear.

Support this statement with at least three sentences.

Paragraph 5. Provide a summary of your narrative.

Restate your fear in different words from the opening sentence.

47

Writing: Paraphrasing

Paraphrasing means to restate something in your own words.

Directions: Write the following sentences in your own words. The first one has been done for you.

1. He sat alone and watched movies throughout the cold, rainy night.

   All through the damp, chilly evening, the boy watched television by himself.

2. Many animals such as elephants, zebras and tigers live in the grasslands.

   _____

3. In art class, Sarah worked diligently on a clay pitcher, molding and shaping it on the pottery wheel.

   Answers will vary.

4. The scientists frantically searched for a cure for the new disease that threatened the entire world population.

   _____

5. Quietly, the detective crept around the abandoned building, hoping to find the missing man.

   _____

6. The windmill turned lazily in the afternoon breeze.

   _____

48

Writing: Paraphrasing

Directions: Using synonyms and different word order, paraphrase the following paragraphs. The first one has been done for you.

Some of the Earth's resources, such as oil and coal, can be used only once. We should always, therefore, be careful how we use them. Some materials that are made from natural resources, including metal, glass and paper, can be reused. This is called recycling.

Many natural resources, including coal and oil, can be used only one time. For this reason, it is necessary to use them wisely. There are other materials made from resources of the Earth that can be recycled, or used again. Materials that can be recycled include metal, glass and paper.

Recycling helps to conserve the limited resources of our land. For example, there are only small amounts of gold and silver ores in the earth. If we can recycle these metals, less of the ores need to be mined. While there is much more aluminum ore in the earth, recycling is still important. It takes less fuel energy to recycle aluminum than it does to make the metal from ore. Therefore, recycling aluminum helps to conserve fuel.

Answers will vary.

It is impossible to get minerals and fossil fuels from the earth without causing damage to its surface. In the past, people did not think much about making these kinds of changes to the Earth. They did not think about how these actions would affect the future. As a result, much of the land around mines was left useless and ugly. This is not necessary, because such land can be restored to its former beauty.

_____

49

Reading Skills: Skimming and Scanning

Skimming is reading quickly to get a general idea of what a reading selection is about. When skimming, look for headings and key words to give you an overall idea of what you are reading.

Scanning is looking for certain words to find facts or answer questions. When scanning, read or think of questions first.

Directions: Scan the paragraphs below to find the answers to the questions. Then look for specific words that will help you locate the answers. For example, in the second question, scan for the word **smallest**.

There are many different units to measure time. Probably the smallest unit that you use is the second, and the longest unit is the year. While 100 years seems like a very long time to us, in the history of the Earth, it is a smaller amount of time than one second is in a person's entire lifetime.

To describe the history of the Earth, scientists use geologic time. Even a million years is a fairly short period in geologic time. Much of the known history of the Earth is described in terms of tens or even hundreds of millions of years. Scientists believe that our planet is about 4,600 million years old. Since a thousand million is a billion, the Earth is said to be 4.6 billion years old.

1. What kind of time is used to describe the history of the Earth?

   geologic time

2. For the average person, what is the smallest unit of time used?

   the second

3. In millions of years, how old do scientists believe the Earth is?

   4,600 million years

4. How would you express that in billions of years?

   4.6 billion years

50

Reading Skills: Author's Purpose

An **author's purpose** is the reason why he/she writes a particular story or book. The author usually wants to entertain, inform or persuade the reader. Sometimes the author can have more than one purpose.

Directions: Read each paragraph. Determine the author's purpose for writing it, and write one or more of the following—**inform, entertain** or **persuade**.

1. In planning for the wise use of our natural resources, it is helpful for people to know the kind of resource they are using. There are, in general, two groups—renewable and non-renewable resources. Renewable resources, such as plants, can be replaced as they are used. Non-renewable resources include fossil fuels and minerals, which cannot be replaced.

Purpose: _____inform_____

2. It is vitally important that each of us acts now to save our natural resources. The future of our planet depends on it. We must not allow any of these resources to be wasted. Write to your senators today, urging them to pass laws that will ensure that there will be plenty of fuel and clean air and water for future generations.

Purpose: _____persuade_____

3. Mother Nature needs you! After millions of years of caring for the needs of humans, Mother Nature now needs our help. She is choking from the polluted air, and her face is scarred and dirtied. So do your part to help your mother—keep the air and waterways clean, and remember to recycle.

Purpose: _____entertain_____

51

Reading Skills: Author's Purpose

Directions: Read the following speeches and write if the speaker is entertaining, informing or persuading his/her audience.

1. Attention fair-goers! For your enjoyment this evening, we have the new band, "Change of Mind," to dazzle you! Straight from Los Angeles, this band has a new sound that will knock you over! Join me in welcoming "Change of Mind"!

Purpose: _____entertaining_____

2. My friends, the time has come for us to join the fight against this deadly disease. We must commit both ourselves and our dollars to eradicate this disease before it reaches epidemic proportions. Don't procrastinate and find that you regret it later. Please donate to our fund.

Purpose: _____persuading_____

3. This year was an excellent one for our company. We created 10 new products and made over $5 billion in profit. We will begin expanding within three months and foresee the creation of 2,000 new jobs.

Purpose: _____informing_____

Write a persuasive paragraph about a rule you believe should be changed. Be sure to provide several supporting sentences.

Answers will vary.

52

Using the Right Resources

Directions: Decide where you would look to find information on the following topics. After each question, write one or more of the following references:

- **almanac** — contains tables and charts of statistics and information
- **atlas** — collection of maps
- **card/computer catalog** — library resource showing available books by topic, title or author
- **dictionary** — contains alphabetical listing of words with their meanings, pronunciations and origins
- **encyclopedia** — set of books or CD-ROM with general information on many subjects
- **Readers' Guide to Periodical Literature** — an index of articles in magazines and newspapers
- **thesaurus** — contains synonyms and antonyms of words

1. What is the capital of The Netherlands? _____atlas, encyclopedia_____
2. What form of government is practiced there? _____almanac, encyclopedia_____
3. What languages are spoken there? _____almanac, encyclopedia_____
4. What is the meaning of the word **indigenous**? _____dictionary, thesaurus_____
5. Where would you find information on conservation? _card/computer catalog, encyclopedia, Readers' Guide to Periodical Literature_
6. What is a synonym for **catastrophe**? _____thesaurus_____
7. Where would you find a review of the play *Cats*? _Readers' Guide to Periodical Literature_
8. Where would you find statistics on the annual rainfall in the Sahara Desert? _____almanac_____
9. What is the origin of the word **plentiful**? _____dictionary_____
10. What are antonyms for the word **plentiful**? _____thesaurus_____
11. Where would you find statistics for the number of automobiles manufactured in the United States last year? _____almanac_____

53

Review

Directions: Read the paragraph, then follow the directions.

According to one estimate, 75 percent of all fresh water on the Earth is in the form of ice. The polar regions of the Earth are almost completely covered by ice. In some places, the ice is more than 8,000 feet thick. If all of this ice were spread out evenly, the Earth would be covered with a 100-foot-thick layer of ice. Although ice is not an important source of fresh water today, it could be in the future. Some people have proposed towing large, floating masses of ice to cities to help keep up with the demand for fresh water.

1. Complete the outline of the paragraph. Sample answers:

Title: _Using Ice for Fresh Water_

Main Topic: I. 75 percent of fresh water on Earth is ice.

Subtopics: A. _The polar regions have the largest source of ice._

B. _Ice could be an important source of fresh water in the future._

2. Check the most appropriate generalization:
   - [X] Ice is the most plentiful source of fresh water.
   - [ ] Ice is important to the future.

3. Paraphrase the first sentence by restating it in your own words.

_____Answer will vary._____

4. Is the author's purpose to inform, entertain or persuade?

to inform

5. Where would you look to find information on the polar ice caps?

an encyclopedia and/or an almanac

54

Review

Directions: Read the paragraph, then follow the directions.

Constellations are groups of stars that have been given names. They often represent an animal, person or object. One of the easiest constellations to identify is the Big Dipper, which is shaped like a spoon. Once the Big Dipper is located, it is easy to see Cassiopeia (a W), the Little Dipper (an upside-down spoon) and the North Star. The North Star's scientific name is Polaris, and it is the last star in the handle of the Little Dipper. Other constellations include Orion the hunter, Gemini the twins, Canis Major the dog and Pegasus the winged horse. Many ancient cultures, including the Greeks and Native Americans, used the position of the stars to guide them. They also planned daily life activities, such as planting, hunting and harvesting, by the path the constellations made through the sky. For thousands of years, humans have gazed at the sky, fascinated by the millions of stars and imagining pictures in the night.

The Constellation Orion

1. Complete the outline of the paragraph. Sample answers:

Title: _Constellations_

Main Topic: I. _Constellations are groups of stars that represent something._

Subtopics: A. _How to locate a few of the constellations_

B. _The meaning of constellations to ancient Greeks and Native Americans_

2. In three sentences, summarize the paragraph.

Sentences will vary.

3. What is the author's purpose? _to inform_

4. Under which topics would you look to find more information on constellations?

astronomy   _Greek mythology_   _Native American star legends_

55

Review

Directions: Imagine you are making a speech about one of your hobbies. Complete an outline of the speech.

Title: _____

Main Topic: I. _____

Subtopics: A. _____

B. _____

Who is your audience? _____

Is it appropriately written for that audience? _____

Are you trying to inform, entertain ___

In the space belo...   Answers will vary.

_____
_____
_____
_____
_____
_____
_____
_____
_____

56

Comprehension: Colonists Come to America

After Christopher Columbus discovered America in 1492, many people wanted to come live in the new land. During the 17th and 18th centuries, a great many Europeans, especially the English, left their countries and settled along the Atlantic Coast of North America between Florida and Canada. Some came to make a better life for themselves. Others, particularly the Pilgrims, the Puritans and the Quakers, came for religious freedom.

A group of men who wanted gold and other riches from the new land formed the London Company. They asked the king of England for land in America and for permission to found a colony. They founded Jamestown, the first permanent English settlement in America, in 1607. They purchased ships and supplies, and located people who wanted to settle in America.

The voyage to America took about eight weeks and was very dangerous. Often, fierce winds blew the wooden ships off course. Many were wrecked. The ships were crowded and dirty. Frequently, passengers became ill, and some died. Once in America, the early settlers faced even more hardships.

Directions: Answer these questions about the colonists coming to America.

1. How long did it take colonists to travel from England to America? _8 weeks_

2. Name three groups that came to America to find religious freedom.
   1) _Pilgrims_ 2) _Puritans_ 3) _Quakers_

3. Why was the London Company formed? _to ask the king of England if they could found a colony in America_

4. What was Jamestown? _the first permanent English settlement in America_

5. Why was the voyage to America dangerous? _Many ships wrecked. They were crowded and dirty, and passengers became ill._

57

Recalling Details: Early Colonial Homes

When the first colonists landed in America, they had to find shelter quickly. Their first homes were crude bark and mud huts, log cabins or dugouts, which were simply caves dug into the hillsides. As soon as possible, the settlers sought to replace these temporary shelters with comfortable houses.

Until the late 17th century, most of the colonial homes were simple in style. Almost all of the New England colonists—those settling in the northern areas of Massachusetts, Connecticut, Rhode Island and New Hampshire—used wood in building their permanent homes. Some of the buildings had thatched roofs. However, they caught fire easily, and so were replaced by wooden shingles. The outside walls also were covered with wooden shingles to make the homes warmer and less drafty.

In the middle colonies—New York, Pennsylvania, New Jersey and Delaware—the Dutch and German colonists often made brick or stone homes that were two-and-a-half or three-and-a-half stories high. Many southern colonists—those living in Virginia, Maryland, North Carolina, South Carolina and Georgia—lived on large farms called plantations. Their homes were usually made of brick.

In the 18th century, some colonists became wealthy enough to replace their simple homes with mansions, often like those being built by the wealthy class in England. They were called Georgian houses because they were popular during the years that Kings George I, George II and George III ruled England. Most were made of brick. They usually featured columns, ornately carved doors and elaborate gardens.

Directions: Answer these questions about early colonial homes.

1. What were the earliest homes of the colonists? _bark and mud huts, log cabins, dugouts_

2. What were the advantages of using wooden shingles? _They didn't catch fire as easily as thatched roofs._

3. What did Dutch and German colonists use to build their homes? _brick and stone_

4. What were Georgian homes? _mansions with columns, ornate doors and elaborate gardens_

58

Recalling Details: The Colonial Kitchen

The most important room in the home of a colonial family was the kitchen. Sometimes it was the only room in the home. The most important element of the kitchen was the fireplace. Fire was essential to the colonists, and they were careful to keep one burning at all times. Before the man of the house went to bed, he would make sure that the fire was carefully banked so it would burn all night. In the morning, he would blow the glowing embers into flame again with a bellows. If the fire went out, one of the children would be sent to a neighbor's for hot coals. Because there were no matches, it would sometimes take a half hour to light a new fire, using flint, steel and tinder.

The colonial kitchen, quite naturally, was centered around the fireplace. One or two large iron broilers hung over the hot coals for cooking the family meals. Above the fireplace, a large musket and powder horn were kept for protection in the event of an attack and to hunt deer and other game. Also likely to be found near the fireplace was a butter churn, where cream from the family's cow was beaten until yellow flakes of butter appeared.

The furniture in the kitchen—usually benches, a table and chairs—were made by the man or men in the family. It was very heavy and not very comfortable. The colonial family owned few eating utensils—no forks and only a few spoons, also made by members of the family. The dishes included pewter plates, "trenchers"—wooden bowls with handles—and wooden mugs.

Directions: Answer these questions about the colonial kitchen.

1. What was the most important element of the colonial kitchen? _fireplace_

2. In colonial days, why was it important to keep a fire burning in the fireplace? _There were no matches, and fires were hard to start._

3. Name two uses of the musket.
   1) _hunting_ 2) _protection_

4. Who made most of the furniture in the early colonial home? _men in the family_

59

Sequencing: Spinning

Most of the colonists could not afford to buy clothes sent over from Europe. Instead, the women and girls, particularly in the New England colonies, spent much time spinning thread and weaving cloth to make their own clothing. They raised sheep for wool and grew flax for linen.

In August, the flax was ready to be harvested and made into linen thread. The plants were pulled up and allowed to dry. Then the men pulled the seed pods from the stalks, bundled the stalks and soaked them in a stream for about five days. The flax next had to be taken out, cleaned and dried. To get the linen fibers from the tough bark and heavy wooden core, the stalks had to be pounded and crushed. Finally, the fibers were pulled through the teeth of a brush called a "hatchel" to comb out the short and broken fibers. The long fibers were spun into linen thread on a spinning wheel.

The spinning wheel was low, so a woman sat down to spin. First, she put flax in the hollow end of a slender stick, called the spindle, at one end of the spinning wheel. It was connected by a belt to a larger wheel at the other end. The woman turned the wheel by stepping on a pedal. As it turned, the spindle also turned, twisting the flax into thread. The woman constantly dipped her fingers into water to moisten the flax and keep it from breaking. The linen thread came out through a hole in the side of the spindle. It was bleached and put away to be woven into pieces of cloth.

Directions: Number in order the steps to make linen thread from flax.

_7_ The woman sat at the spinning wheel and put flax in the spindle.

_3_ Seed pods were pulled from the stalks; stalks were bundled and soaked.

_1_ In August, the flax was ready to be harvested and made into thread.

_4_ The stalks were pounded and crushed to get the linen fibers.

_11_ The thread was bleached and put away to be woven into cloth.

_5_ The short fibers were separated out with a "hatchel."

_9_ The woman dipped her fingers into water to moisten the flax.

_6_ The long fibers were spun into linen thread on a spinning wheel.

_8_ The woman turned the wheel by stepping on a pedal, twisting the flax into thread.

_2_ The plants were pulled up and allowed to dry.

_10_ The linen thread came out through a hole in the side of the spindle.

60

Recalling Details: Clothing in Colonial Times

The clothing of the colonists varied from the north to the south, accounting for the differences not only in climate, but also in the religions and ancestries of the settlers. The clothes seen most often in the early New England colonies where the Puritans settled were very plain and simple. The materials—wool and linen—were warm and sturdy.

The Puritans had strict rules about clothing. There were no bright colors, jewelry, ruffles or lace. A Puritan woman wore a long-sleeved gray dress with a big white color, cuffs, apron and cap. A Puritan man wore long woolen stockings and baggy leather "breeches," which were knee-length trousers. Adults and children dressed in the same style of clothing.

In the middle colonies, the clothing ranged from the simple clothing of the Quakers to the colorful, loose-fitting outfits of the Dutch colonists. Dutch women wore more colorful outfits than Puritan women, with many petticoats and fur trim. The men had silver buckles on their shoes and wore big hats decked with curling feathers.

In the southern colonies, where there were no religious restrictions against fancy clothes, wealthy men wore brightly colored breeches and coats of velvet and satin sent from England. The women's gowns also were made of rich materials and were decorated with ruffles, ribbons and lace. The poorer people wore clothes similar to the simple dress of the New England Puritans.

Directions: Answer these questions about clothing in colonial times.

1. Why did the clothing of the colonists vary from the north to the south? _differences in climate, religions and ancestries_

2. Why did the Puritans wear very plain clothing? _They had very strict rules and religious restrictions._

3. What was the nationality of many settlers in the middle colonies? _Dutch_

4. From what country did wealthy southern colonists obtain their clothing? _England_

61

Recalling Details: Venn Diagrams

A **Venn diagram** is used to chart information that shows similarities and differences between two things. The outer part of each circle shows the differences. The intersecting part of the circles shows the similarities.

Example:

Basketball — Played on a court, Points scored through baskets, Five players on a team

(intersection) Played with a ball, Two teams, Professional sport

Baseball — Played on a diamond, Points scored through runs, Nine players on a team

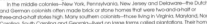

Directions: Complete the Venn diagram below. Think of at least three things to write in the outer part of each circle (diff...) ...gs to write in the intersecting part (similarities).

Sample answers:

Colonial Kitchen — Furniture made by family, No matches, Fireplace, Butter made with churn

(intersection) Table and chairs, Most important room in house

Your Kitchen — Furniture bought at store, Matches, Oven, Butter bought at store

62

Comprehension: Colonial Schools

In early colonial days, there were no schools or teachers. Children learned what they could at home from their parents, but often their parents couldn't read or write either. Later, some women in the New England colonies began teaching in their homes. These first schools were known as "dame schools." Often the books used in these schools were not books at all, but rather "hornbooks"—flat, paddle-shaped wooden boards with the alphabet or Lord's Prayer on the front.

In 1647, a law was passed in the New England colonies requiring every town of 50 or more families to establish an elementary school. By the 1700s, one-room log schoolhouses were common. Children of all ages studied together under one strict schoolmaster. They attended school six days a week, from 7:00 or 8:00 in the morning until 4:00 or 5:00 in the afternoon. Their only textbooks were the Bible and the *New England Primer*, which contained the alphabet, spelling words, poems and questions about the Bible.

Like the New England colonies, the middle colonies also established schools. However, there were few schools in the southern colonies, where most of the people lived on widely separated farms. Wealthy plantation owners hired private teachers from England to teach their children, but the children of poor families received no education.

Directions: Answer these questions about colonial schools.

1. What was a "hornbook"? <u>flat wooden boards with the alphabet or Lord's Prayer on the front</u>

2. What was required by the law passed in the New England colonies in 1647? <u>Every town with 50 or more families had to establish an elementary school.</u>

3. During the 1700s, what textbooks were used in the New England schools? <u>the Bible and the *New England Primer*</u>

4. Why was it hard to establish schools in the southern colonies? <u>Most people lived on widely seperated farms.</u>

63

Compare/Contrast: Schools

Directions: Think about the differences and similarities between colonial and modern schools. Use the chart below to help organize your ideas. Then, write a paragraph discussing the similarities and a paragraph discussing the differences. The topic sentences have been written for you.

Sample answers:

Similarities	Differences
• studied alphabet, spelling, poems	• one-room log schoolhouses
• one teacher in the room	• six-day school week
	• 8-9 hour school day
	• only two textbooks

There are several similarities between colonial schools and schools today.

Answers will vary.

Although there are ... and modern schools, there are also many differences.

64

Comprehension: Religion in New England

Many New England colonists had come to America for religious freedom. Religion was very important to them. One of the first buildings erected in any new settlement was a church, or meetinghouse. They were generally in the center of town and were used for public meetings of all kinds. These early meetinghouses were plain, unpainted wood buildings. Later churches were larger and more elaborate. They were usually painted white and had tall, graceful bell towers rising from the roof.

Although they came to America to have freedom of worship, the Puritans thought that everyone in the colonies should worship the same way they did. Because there were so many of them, the Puritans controlled the government in much of New England. They were the only ones allowed to vote, and they passed very strict laws. Lawbreakers received harsh punishments. For example, someone caught lying might be forced to stand in the town square for hours locked in a pillory—wooden boards with holes cut in them for the head and hands. For other minor offenses, the offender was tied to a whipping post and given several lashes with a whip.

Except in cases of extreme illness, everyone in the New England colonies had to attend church on Sunday. The minister stood in a pulpit high above the pews to deliver his sermon, which could last four or five hours. The people sat on hard, straight-backed pews. In the winter, there was no heat, so church members brought foot warmers from home to use during the long services. In many churches, a "tithingman" walked up and down the aisles carrying a long stick. On one end there were feathers attached; the other end had a knob. If anyone dozed off, the tithingman would tickle him or her with the feathers. If this did not rouse the offender, he would thump them soundly with the knob.

Directions: Answer these questions about religion in the colonies.

1. The main idea is:

   ☒ Many New England colonists had come to America for religious freedom, and religion was very important to them.

   ☐ One of the first buildings erected in any new settlement was a church.

2. Which religious group exercised a lot of power in the New England colonies? <u>Puritans</u>

3. What was a pillory? <u>wooden boards with holes cut for the head and hands</u>

4. What was the only acceptable excuse for missing Sunday church services in the New England colonies? <u>extreme illness</u>

5. What was the job of the tithingman? <u>to keep people awake in church</u>

65

Writing: Problem and Solution

Directions: Follow the instructions below.

1. Think of a problem the Colonial Americans may have encountered. Write a paragraph about this problem. In the paragraph, be sure to state the problem, then discuss why it would have been a problem for the colonists.

Answers will vary.

2. Think about a solution to the problem above. Write a paragraph outlining your ideas for the solution. Remember to state the solution to the problem and then your ideas to solve the problem.

66

Writing: Problem and Solution

Directions: Write a two-paragraph personal narrative about a problem you are experiencing. In the first paragraph, state reasons why it is a problem. In the second paragraph, write a possible solution to your problem.

Answers will vary.

Directions: Think of anything that could go wrong with your solution. Write about it below.

67

Review

Many great colonists made an impact on American history. Among them was Benjamin Franklin, who left his mark as a printer, author, inventor, scientist and statesman. He has been called "the wisest American."

Franklin was born in Boston in 1706, one of 13 children in a very religious Puritan household. Although he had less than four years of formal education, his tremendous appetite for books served him well. At age 12, he became an apprentice printer at *The New England Courant* and soon began writing articles that poked fun at Boston society.

In 1723, Franklin ran away to Philadelphia, where he started his own newspaper. He was very active in the Philadelphia community. He operated a bookstore and was named postmaster. He also helped to establish a library, a fire company, a college, an insurance company and a hospital. His well-known *Poor Richard's Almanac* was first printed in 1732.

Over the years, Franklin maintained an interest in science and mechanics, leading to such inventions as a fireplace stove and bifocal lenses. In 1752, he gained world fame with his kite-and-key experiment, which proved that lightning was a form of electricity.

Franklin was an active supporter of the colonies throughout the Revolutionary War. He helped to write and was a signer of the Declaration of Independence in 1776. In his later years, he skillfully represented America in Europe, helping to work out a peace treaty with Great Britain.

Directions: Answer these questions about Benjamin Franklin.

1. The main idea is:

   ☐ Many great colonists made an impact on American history.

   ☒ Benjamin Franklin was a great colonist who left his mark as a printer, author, inventor, scientist and statesman.

2. How did Benjamin Franklin gain world fame? <u>his kite-and-key experiment</u>

3. What did Franklin sign and help to write? <u>Declaration of Independence</u>

4. Number in order the following accomplishments of Benjamin Franklin.

   <u>6</u> Served as representative of America in Europe

   <u>3</u> Began printing *Poor Richard's Almanac*

   <u>4</u> Experimented with electricity

   <u>2</u> Started his own newspaper

   <u>5</u> Helped to write and sign the Declaration of Independence

   <u>1</u> Served as apprentice printer on *The New England Courant*

68

Review

Directions: Match each item with its description. If necessary, review the section on colonial times.

a. hornbooks		j	year Columbus sailed to America
b. 1647		m	schools where New England women taught in their homes
c. pillory		g	man who kept worshippers awake during Sunday services
d. Ben Franklin		l	plants harvested for linen
e. plantations		a	paddle-shaped wooden boards with text on them
f. 1776		b	law written in this year required towns of 50 or more to establish a school
g. tithingman		c	punishment rack with holes for head and hands
h. spinning wheel		k	wooden bowls with handles
i. hatchel		d	author of *Poor Richard's Almanac*
j. 1492		e	large farms in the South
k. trenchers		h	wooden machine used to spin wool or flax into thread
l. flax		i	used to comb out the short and broken flax fibers
m. dame schools		f	year Declaration of Independence was signed

69

Recalling Details: The Earth's Atmosphere

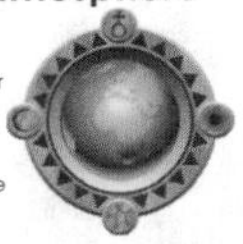

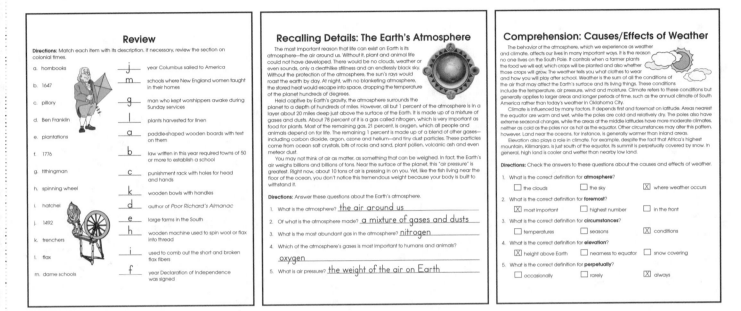

The most important reason that life can exist on Earth is its atmosphere—the air around us. Without it, plant and animal life could not have developed. There would be no clouds, weather or even sounds, only a deathlike stillness and an endlessly black sky. Without the protection of the atmosphere, the sun's rays would roast the earth by day. At night, with no blanketing atmosphere, the stored heat would escape into space, dropping the temperature of the planet hundreds of degrees.

Held captive by Earth's gravity, the atmosphere surrounds the planet to a depth of hundreds of miles. However, all but 1 percent of the atmosphere is in a layer about 20 miles deep just above the surface of the Earth. It is made up of a mixture of gases and dusts. About 78 percent of it is a gas called nitrogen, which is very important as food for plants. Most of the remaining gas, 21 percent, is oxygen, which all people and animals depend on for life. The remaining 1 percent is made up of a blend of other gases—including carbon dioxide, argon, ozone and helium—and tiny dust particles. These particles come from ocean salt crystals, bits of rocks and sand, plant pollen, volcanic ash and even meteor dust.

You may not think of air as matter, as something that can be weighed. In fact, the Earth's air weighs billions and billions of tons. Near the surface of the planet, this "air pressure" is greatest. Right now, about 10 tons of air is pressing in on you. Yet, like the fish living near the floor of the ocean, you don't notice this tremendous weight because your body is built to withstand it.

Directions: Answer these questions about the Earth's atmosphere.

1. What is the atmosphere? the air around us
2. Of what is the atmosphere made? a mixture of gases and dusts
3. What is the most abundant gas in the atmosphere? nitrogen
4. Which of the atmosphere's gases is most important to humans and animals? oxygen
5. What is air pressure? the weight of the air on Earth

70

Comprehension: Causes/Effects of Weather

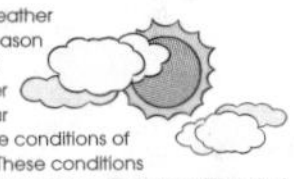

The behavior of the atmosphere, which we experience as weather and climate, affects our lives in many important ways. It is the reason no one lives on the South Pole. It controls when a farmer plants the food we will eat, which crops will be planted and also whether those crops will grow. The weather tells you what clothes to wear and how you will play after school. Weather is the sum of all the conditions of the air that may affect the Earth's surface and its living things. These conditions include the temperature, air pressure, wind and moisture. Climate refers to these conditions but generally applies to larger areas and longer periods of time, such as the annual climate of South America rather than today's weather in Oklahoma City.

Climate is influenced by many factors. It depends first and foremost on latitude. Areas nearest the equator are warm and wet, while the poles are cold and relatively dry. The poles also have extreme seasonal changes, while the areas at the middle latitudes have more moderate climates, neither as cold as the poles nor as hot as the equator. Other circumstances may alter this pattern, however. Land near the oceans, for instance, is generally warmer than inland areas.

Elevation also plays a role in climate. For example, despite the fact that Africa's highest mountain, Kilimanjaro, is just south of the equator, its summit is perpetually covered by snow. In general, high land is cooler and wetter than nearby low land.

Directions: Check the answers to these questions about the causes and effects of weather.

1. What is the correct definition for **atmosphere**?
   ☐ the clouds ☐ the sky ☒ where weather occurs
2. What is the correct definition for **foremost**?
   ☒ most important ☐ highest number ☐ in the front
3. What is the correct definition for **circumstances**?
   ☐ temperatures ☐ seasons ☒ conditions
4. What is the correct definition for **elevation**?
   ☒ height above Earth ☐ nearness to equator ☐ snow covering
5. What is the correct definition for **perpetually**?
   ☐ occasionally ☐ rarely ☒ always

71

Main Idea/Recalling Details: Weather

People have always searched the sky for clues about upcoming weather. Throughout the ages, farmers and sailors have looked to the winds and clouds for signs of approaching storms. But no real understanding of the weather could be achieved without a scientific study of the atmosphere. Such a study depends on being able to measure certain conditions, including pressure, temperature and moisture levels.

A true scientific examination of weather, therefore, was not possible until the development of accurate measuring instruments, beginning in the 17th century. Meteorology—the science of studying the atmosphere—was born in 1643 with the invention of the barometer, which measures atmospheric pressure. The liquid-in-glass thermometer, the hygrometer to measure humidity—the mount of moisture in the air—and the weather map also were invented during the 1600s.

With the measurement of these basic elements, scientists began to work out the relationships between these and other atmospheric conditions, such as wind, clouds and rainfall. Still, their observations failed to show an overall picture of the weather. Such complete weather reporting had to wait two centuries for the rapid transfer of information made possible by the invention of the telegraph during the 1840s.

Today, the forecasts of meteorologists are an international effort. There are thousands of weather stations around the world, both at land and at sea. Upper-level observations are also made by weather balloons and satellites, which continuously send photographs back to earth. All of this information is relayed to national weather bureaus, where meteorologists plot it on graphs and analyze it. The information is then given to the public through newspapers and television and radio stations.

Directions: Answer these questions about studying the weather.

1. The main idea is:
   ☐ People have always searched the sky for clues about upcoming weather.
   ☒ A real understanding of weather depends on measuring conditions such as pressure, temperature and moisture levels.
2. List three kinds of instruments used to measure atmospheric conditions, and tell what conditions they measure.
   1) barometer — atmospheric pressure
   2) hygrometer — humidity
   3) liquid-in-glass thermometer — temperature
3. During what century were many of these measuring instruments invented? 17th
4. Name two things used for upper-level observations.
   1) weather balloon 2) satellite

72

Comprehension: Hurricanes

The characteristics of a hurricane are powerful winds, driving rain and raging seas. Although a storm must have winds blowing at least 74 miles an hour to be classified as a hurricane, it is not unusual to have winds above 150 miles per hour. The entire storm system can be 500 miles in diameter, with lines of clouds that spiral toward a center called the "eye." Within the eye itself, which is about 15 miles across, the air is actually calm and cloudless. But this eye is enclosed by a towering wall of thick clouds where the storm's heaviest rains and highest winds are found.

All hurricanes begin in the warm seas and moist winds of the tropics. They form in either of two narrow bands to the north and south of the equator. For weeks, the blistering sun beats down on the ocean water. Slowly, the air above the sea becomes heated and begins to swirl. More hot, moist air is pulled skyward. Gradually, this circle grows larger and spins faster. As the hot, moist air at the top is cooled, great rain clouds are formed. The storm's fury builds until it moves over land or a cold area of the ocean where its supply of heat and moisture is finally cut off.

Hurricanes that strike North America usually form over the Atlantic Ocean. West coast storms are less dangerous because they tend to head out over the Pacific Ocean rather than toward land. The greatest damage usually comes from the hurricanes that begin in the western Pacific, because they often batter heavily populated regions.

Directions: Answer these questions about hurricanes.

1. What is necessary for a storm to be classified as a hurricane? winds blowing at least 74 miles an hour
2. What is the "eye" of the hurricane? lines of clouds that spiral toward the center
3. Where do hurricanes come from? warm seas and moist winds of the tropics
4. How does a hurricane finally die down? It moves over land or a cold area of the ocean where its supply of heat and moisture is cut off.
5. Why do hurricanes formed in the western Pacific cause the most damage? They often batter heavily populated areas.

73

Comprehension: Tornadoes

Tornadoes, which are also called twisters, occur more frequently than hurricanes, but they are smaller storms. The zigzag path of a tornado averages about 16 miles in length and only about a quarter of a mile wide. But the tornado is, pound for pound, the more severe storm. When one touches the ground, it leaves a trail of total destruction.

The winds in a tornado average about 200 miles per hour. At the center of the funnel-shaped cloud of a tornado is a partial vacuum. In combination with the high winds, this is what makes the storm so destructive. Its force is so great that a tornado can drive a piece of straw into a tree. The extremely low atmospheric pressure that accompanies the storm can cause a building to actually explode.

Unlike hurricanes, tornadoes are formed over land. They are most likely to occur over the central plains of the United States, especially in the spring and early summer months. Conditions for a tornado arise when warm, moist air from the south becomes trapped under colder, heavier air from the north. When the surfaces of the two air masses touch, rain clouds form and a thunderstorm begins. At first, only a rounded bulge hangs from the bottom of the cloud. It gradually gets longer until it forms a column reaching toward the ground. The tornado is white from the moisture when it first forms, but turns black as it sucks up dirt and trash.

Directions: Circle **True** or **False** for these statements about tornadoes.

1. The tornado is a stronger storm than the hurricane. (True) False
2. The path of a tornado usually covers hundreds of miles. True (False)
3. Like the eye of a hurricane, the center of a tornado is calm. True (False)
4. Tornadoes are most likely to occur in the central plains of the United States during the spring and early summer months. (True) False
5. High atmospheric pressure usually accompanies a tornado. True (False)

74

Comprehension: Thunderstorms

With warm weather comes the threat of thunderstorms. The rapid growth of the majestic thunderhead cloud and the damp, cool winds that warn of an approaching storm are familiar in most regions of the world. In fact, it has been estimated that at any given time 1,800 such storms are in progress around the globe.

As with hurricanes and tornadoes, thunderstorms are formed when a warm, moist air mass meets with a cold air mass. Before long, bolts of lightning streak across the sky, and thunder booms. It is not entirely understood how lightning is formed. It is known that a positive electrical charge builds near the top of the cloud, and a negative charge forms at the bottom. When enough force builds up, a powerful current of electricity zigzags down an electrically charged pathway between the two, causing the flash of lightning.

The clap of thunder you hear after a lightning flash is created by rapidly heated air that expands as the lightning passes through it. The distant rumbling is caused by the thunder's sound waves bouncing back and forth within clouds or between mountains. When thunderstorms rumble through an area, many people begin to worry about tornadoes. But they need to be just as fearful of thunderstorms. In fact, lightning kills more people than any other severe weather condition. In 1988, lightning killed 68 people in the United States, while tornadoes killed 32.

Directions: Answer these questions about thunderstorms.

1. How many thunderstorms are estimated to be occurring at any given time around the world?
   1,800

2. When are thunderstorms formed?
   when a warm, moist air mass meets a cold air mass

3. What causes thunder?
   rapidly heated air that expands as lightning passes through it

4. On average, which causes more deaths, lightning or tornadoes?
   lightning

75

Venn Diagram: Storms

Directions: Complete the Venn diagram below. Think of at least three things to write in the outer parts of each circle and at least three things to write in the intersecting parts.

Sample answers:

Hurricanes

Occur most often off Atlantic Ocean
Formed over warm seas
"Eye" in center is peaceful

Strong winds
Warm, moist air

Rain

Tornadoes

Occur most often in central plains of U.S.
Funnel cloud
Vacuum in center is destructive

Occur in spring and summer

Occur anywhere in U.S.
Thunder and lightning

Thunderstorms

76

Writing: Weather

Directions: Write an essay about your own experience in a severe storm. Write at least three paragraphs, and include the following:

What type of storm was it?
Where were you?
How did you feel?

Answers will vary.

Writing Checklist

Reread your essay carefully.

☐ My essay makes sense.
☐ There are no jumps in ideas.
☐ I used correct punctuation.
☐ My essay is interesting.

☐ I have a good opening and ending.
☐ I used correct spelling.
☐ My essay is well-organized.

77

Recalling Details: Lightning Safety Rules

Lightning causes more fire damage to forests and property than anything else. More importantly, it kills more people than any other weather event. It is important to know what to do—and what not to do—during a thunderstorm. Here are some important rules to remember:

• **Don't** go outdoors.
• **Don't** go near open doors or windows, fireplaces, radiators, stoves, metal pipes, sinks or plug-in electrical appliances.
• **Don't** use the telephone, as lightning could strike the wires outside.
• **Don't** handle metal objects, such as fishing poles or golf clubs.
• **Don't** go into the water or ride in small boats.
• **Do** stay in an automobile if you are traveling. Cars offer excellent protection.
• **Don't** take laundry off the clothesline.
• **Do** look for shelter if you are outdoors. If there is no shelter, stay away from the highest object in the area. If there are only a few trees nearby, it is best to crouch in the open, away from the trees at a distance greater than the height of the nearest tree. If you are in an area with many trees, avoid the tallest tree. Look for shorter ones.
• **Don't** take shelter near wire fences or clotheslines, exposed sheds or on a hilltop.
• If your hair stands on end or your skin tingles, lightning may be about to strike you. Immediately crouch down, put your feet together and place your hands over your ears.

Directions: Answer these questions about lightning safety rules.

1. Name two things you should avoid if you are looking for shelter outside.
   1) the highest object in the area
   2) the tallest tree

2. What should you do if, during a thunderstorm, your hair stands up or your skin tingles?
   Immediately crouch down, put your feet together and place your hands over your ears.

78

Main Idea/Comprehension: Rainbows

Although there are some violent, frightening aspects of the weather, there is, of course, considerable beauty, too. The rainbow is one simple, lovely example of nature's atmospheric mysteries.

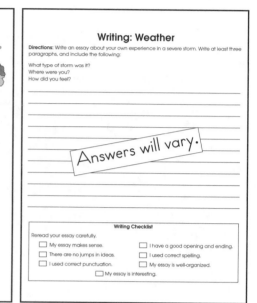

You usually can see a rainbow when the sun comes out after a rain shower or in the fine spray of a waterfall or fountain. Although sunlight appears to be white, it is actually made up of a mixture of colors—all the colors in the rainbow. We see a rainbow because thousands of tiny raindrops act as mirrors and prisms on the sunlight. Prisms are objects that bend light, splitting it into bands of color.

The bands of color form a perfect semicircle. From the top edge to the bottom, the colors are always in the same order--red, orange, yellow, green, indigo and violet. The brightness and width of each band may vary from one minute to the next. You also may notice that the sky framed by the rainbow is lighter than the sky above. This is because the light that forms the blue and violet bands is more bent and spread out than the light that forms the top red band.

You will always see morning rainbows in the west, with the sun behind you. Afternoon rainbows, likewise, are always in the east. To see a rainbow, the sun can be no higher than 42 degrees—nearly halfway up the sky. Sometimes, if the sunlight is strong and the water droplets are very small, you can see a double rainbow. This happens because the light is reflected twice in the water droplets. The color bands are fainter and in reverse order in the second band.

Directions: Answer these questions about rainbows.

1. Check the statement that is the main idea.

☐ Although there are violent, frightening aspects of weather, there is considerable beauty, too.
☒ The rainbow is one simple, lovely example of nature's atmospheric mysteries.

2. What is the correct definition for **semicircle**?
☐ colored circle   ☐ diameter of a circle   ☒ half circle

3. What is a prism? an object that bends light and splits it into bands of color

4. In which direction would you look to see an afternoon rainbow? east

79

Comprehension: Cause and Effect

Directions: Complete the chart by listing the cause and effect of each weather phenomenon.

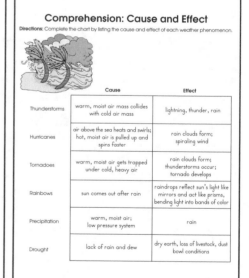

	Cause	Effect
Thunderstorms	warm, moist air mass collides with cold air mass	lightning, thunder, rain
Hurricanes	air above the sea heats and swirls; hot, moist air is pulled up and spins faster	rain clouds form; spiraling wind
Tornadoes	warm, moist air gets trapped under cold, heavy air	rain clouds form; thunderstorms occur; tornado develops
Rainbows	sun comes out after rain	raindrops reflect sun's light like mirrors and act like prisms, bending light into bands of color
Precipitation	warm, moist air; low pressure system	rain
Drought	lack of rain and dew	dry earth, loss of livestock, dust bowl conditions

80

Review

Directions: If necessary, review the section on weather to find the answers to the following questions.

1. Describe the earth's atmosphere. a mixture of gases and dusts that surrounds Earth at a depth of 100 miles

2. The science of studying weather is called meteorology

3. Why is it important for weather forecasting to be an international effort?
Answers will vary but may include: As more people travel, knowledge of weather in other countries becomes important. It is also important to track weather systems.

4. Define **weather** the sum of all the conditions of the air that may affect the Earth's surface and its living things

5. Name three factors that influence climate.
latitude   elevation   proximity to ocean

Sample answers:

6. Describe the following weather phenomena.

a. hurricane powerful winds, driving rain and raging seas

b. tornado warm, moist winds trapped under cold, heavy air that results in a funnel cloud

c. thunderstorm warm, moist air meets a cold air mass which results in rain, thunder and lightning

81

Review

Directions: If necessary, review the section on weather to find answers to the following questions.

1. What atmospheric conditions are necessary for a tornado to form?
warm, moist winds trapped under cold, heavy air

2. Describe how scientists believe lightning is formed.
A positive electrical charge builds near the top of a cloud, and a negative charge builds near the bottom. A current of electricity zigzags down an electrically charged path.

3. How is a rainbow formed?
Tiny raindrops act as mirrors and prisms on sunlight.

4. Research a famous hurricane, such as Iniki or Andrew. Write an informational paragraph about it.

Answers will vary.

Writing Checklist
Reread your paragraph carefully.
- [ ] My paragraph makes sense.
- [ ] I used correct punctuation.
- [ ] There are no jumps in ideas.
- [ ] I have a good opening and ending.
- [ ] I used correct spelling.
- [ ] My paragraph is well-organized.
- [ ] My paragraph is interesting.

82

Recalling Details: The Island Continent

Australia is the only country that fills an entire continent. It is the smallest continent in the world but the sixth largest country. Australia, called the island continent, is totally surrounded by water—the Indian Ocean on the west and south, the Pacific Ocean on the east and the Arafura Sea, which is formed by these two oceans coming together, to the north.

The island continent is, in large part, a very dry, flat land. Yet it supports a magnificent and unusual collection of wildlife. Because of its remoteness, Australia is home to plants and animals that are not found anywhere else in the world. Besides the well-known kangaroo and koala, the strange animals of the continent include the wombat, dingo, kookaburra, emu and, perhaps the strangest of all, the duckbill platypus.

There are many physical features of Australia that also are unique, including the central part of the country known as the "Outback," which consists of three main deserts—the Great Sandy, the Gibson and the Great Victoria. Because much of the country is desert, more than half of all Australians live in large, modern cities along the coast. There are also many people living in the small towns on the edge of the Outback, where there is plenty of grass for raising sheep and cattle. Australia rates first in the world for sheep raising. In fact, there are more than 10 times as many sheep in Australia as there are people!

Directions: Answer these questions about Australia.

1. What are the three large bodies of water that surround Australia?
1) Indian Ocean 2) Pacific Ocean 3) Arafura Sea

2. Besides the kangaroo and the koala, name three other unusual animals found only in Australia. Answers also include: kookaburra and duckbill platypus
1) Wombat 2) Emu 3) Dingo

3. What three deserts make up the "Outback?"
1) Great Sandy 2) Gibson 3) Great Victoria

83

Comprehension: The Aborigines

The native, or earliest known, people of Australia are the Aborigines (ab-ur-IJ-uh-neez). They arrived on the continent from Asia more than 20,000 years ago. Before the Europeans began settling in Australia during the early 1800s, there were about 300,000 Aborigines. But the new settlers brought diseases that killed many of these native people. Today there are only about 125,000 Aborigines living in Australia, many of whom now live in the cities.

The way of life of the Aborigines, who still live like their ancestors, is closely related to nature. They live as hunters and gatherers and do not produce crops or raise livestock. The Aborigines have no permanent settlements, only small camps near watering places. Because they live off the land, they must frequently move about in search of food. They have few belongings and little or no clothing.

Some tribes of Aborigines, especially those that live in the desert, may move 100 times in a year. They might move more than 1,000 miles on foot during that time. These tribes set up temporary homes, such as tents made of bark and igloo-like structures made of grass.

The Aborigines have no written language, but they have developed a system of hand signals. These are used during hunting when silence is necessary and during their elaborate religious ceremonies when talking is forbidden.

Directions: Circle **True** or **False** for these statements about Aborigines.

1. The Aborigines came from Europe to settle in Australia.   True (False)
2. The Aborigines live as hunters and gatherers rather than as farmers.   (True) False
3. The tribes move about often to find jobs.   True (False)
4. The people move often to help them raise their livestock.   True (False)
5. Aborigine tribes always move 200 times a year.   True (False)

84

Main Idea/Comprehension: The Boomerang

The Aborigines have developed a few tools and weapons, including spears, flint knives and the boomerang. The boomerang comes in different shapes and has many uses. This curved throwing stick is used for hunting, playing, digging, cutting and even making music.

You may have seen a boomerang that, when thrown, returns to the thrower. This type of boomerang is sometimes used in duck hunting, but it is most often used as a toy and for sporting contests. It is lightweight—about three-fourths of a pound—and has a big curve in it. However, the boomerang used by the Aborigines for hunting is much heavier and is nearly straight. It does not return to its thrower.

Because of its sharp edges, the boomerang makes a good knife for skinning animals. The Aborigines also use boomerangs as digging sticks, to sharpen stone blades, to start fires and as swords and clubs in fighting. Boomerangs sometimes are used to make music—two clapped together provide rhythmic background for dances. Some make musical sounds when they are pulled across one another.

To throw a boomerang, the thrower grasps it at one end and holds it behind his head. He throws it overhanded, adding a sharp flick of the wrist at the last moment. It is thrown into the wind to make it come back. A skillful thrower can do many tricks with his boomerang. He can make it spin in several circles, or make a figure eight in the air. He can even make it bounce on the ground several times before it soars into the air and returns.

Directions: Answer these questions about boomerangs.

1. The main idea is:
- [ ] The Aborigines have developed a few tools and weapons, including spears, flint knives and the boomerang.
- [X] The boomerang comes in different shapes and has many uses.

2. To make it return, the thrower tosses the boomerang
- [X] into the wind.   - [ ] against the wind.

3. List three uses for the boomerang. Sample answers:
1) hunting
2) playing
3) digging

85

Comprehension: The Kangaroo

Many animals found in Australia are not found anywhere else in the world. Because the island continent was separated from the rest of the world for many years, these animals developed in different ways. Many of the animals in Australia are marsupials. Marsupials are animals whose babies are born underdeveloped and are then carried in a pouch on the mother's body until they are able to care for themselves. The kangaroo is perhaps the best known of the marsupials.

There are 45 kinds of kangaroos, and they come in a variety of sizes. The smallest is the musky rat kangaroo, which is about a foot long, including its hairless tail. It weighs only a pound. The largest is the gray kangaroo, which is more than 9 feet long, counting its tail, and can weigh 200 pounds. When moving quickly, a kangaroo can leap 25 feet and move at 30 miles an hour!

A baby kangaroo, called a joey, is totally helpless at birth. It is only three-quarters of an inch long and weighs but a fraction of an ounce. The newly born joey immediately crawls into its mother's pouch and remains there until it is old enough to be independent—which can be as long as eight months.

Kangaroos eat grasses and plants. They can cause problems for farmers and ranchers in Australia because they compete with cattle for pastures. During a drought, kangaroos may invade ranches and even airports looking for food.

Directions: Answer these questions about kangaroos.

1. What are marsupials? animals whose babies are born underdeveloped and are carried in a pouch on the mother until they can care for themselves
2. What is the smallest kangaroo? musky rat kangaroo
3. What is a baby kangaroo called? joey
4. Why did Australian animals develop differently from other animals? The island continent was separated from the rest of the world for many years.

86

Comprehension: The Koala

The koala lives in eastern Australia in the eucalyptus (you-ca-LIP-tes) forests. These slow, gentle animals hide by day, usually sleeping in the trees. They come out at night to eat. Koalas eat only certain types of eucalyptus leaves. Their entire way of life centers on this unique diet. The koala's digestive system is specially adapted for eating eucalyptus leaves. In fact, to other animals, these leaves are poisonous!

The wooly, round-eared koala looks like a cuddly teddy bear, but it is not related to any bear. It is a marsupial like the kangaroo. And, like the joey, a baby koala requires a lot of care. It will remain constantly in its mother's pouch until it is six months old. After that, a baby koala will ride piggyback on its mother for another month or two, even though it is nearly as big as she is. Koalas have few babies—only one every other year. While in her pouch, the baby koala lives on its mother's milk. After it is big enough to be on its own, the koala will almost never drink anything again.

Oddly, the mother koala's pouch is backwards—the opening is at the bottom. This leads scientists to believe that the koala once lived on the ground and walked on all fours. But at some point, the koala became a tree dweller. This makes an upside-down pouch very awkward! The babies keep from falling to the ground by holding on tightly with their mouths. The mother koala has developed strong muscles around the rim of her pouch that also help

Directions: Answer these questions about koalas.

1. What is the correct definition for **eucalyptus**?
   - ☐ enormous ☒ a type of tree ☐ rain
2. What is the correct definition for **digestive**?
   - ☒ the process in which food is absorbed in the body
   - ☐ the process of finding food
   - ☐ the process of tasting
3. What is the correct definition for **dweller**?
   - ☐ one who climbs ☐ one who eats ☒ one who lives in

87

Comprehension: The Wombat

Another animal unique to Australia is the wombat. The wombat has characteristics in common with other animals. Like the koala, the wombat is also a marsupial with a backwards pouch. The pouch is more practical for the wombat, which lives on the ground rather than in trees. The wombat walks on all fours so the baby is in less danger of falling out.

The wombat resembles a beaver without a tail. With its strong claws, it is an expert digger. It makes long tunnels beneath cliffs and boulders in which it sleeps all day. At night, it comes out to look for food. It has strong, beaver-like teeth to chew through the various plant roots it eats. A wombat's teeth have no roots, like a rodent's. Its teeth keep growing from the inside as they are worn down from the outside.

The wombat, which can be up to 4 feet long and weighs 60 pounds when full grown, eats only grass, plants and roots. It is a shy, quiet and gentle animal that would never attack. But when angered, it has a strong bite and very sharp teeth! And, while wombats don't eat or attack other animals, the many deep burrows they dig to sleep in are often dangerous to the other animals living nearby.

Directions: Answer these questions about the wombat.

1. How is the wombat similar to the koala? It is a marsupial with a backwards pouch.
2. How is the wombat similar to the beaver? It has strong claws to dig and strong teeth to chew through plants.
3. How is the wombat similar to a rodent? Its teeth have no roots but keep growing from the inside as they are worn down from the outside.

88

Comprehension: The Duckbill Platypus

Australia's duckbill platypus is a most unusual animal. It is very strange-looking and has caused a lot of confusion for people studying it. For many years, even scientists did not know how to classify it. The platypus has webbed feet and a bill like a duck. But it doesn't have wings, has fur instead of feathers and has four legs instead of two. The baby platypus gets milk from its mother, like a mammal, but it is hatched from a tough-skinned egg, like a reptile. A platypus also has a poisonous spur on each of its back legs that is like the tip of a viper's fangs. Scientists have put the platypus—along with another strange animal from Australia called the spiny anteater—in a special class of mammal called "monotremes."

The platypus has an amazing appetite! It has been estimated that a full-grown platypus eats about 1,200 earthworms, 50 crayfish and numerous tadpoles and insects every day. The platypus is an excellent swimmer and diver. It dives under the water of a stream and searches the muddy bottom for food.

A mother platypus lays one or two eggs, which are very small—only about an inch long—and leathery in appearance. During the seven to 14 days it takes for the eggs to hatch, the mother never leaves them, not even to eat. The tiny platypus, which is only a half-inch long, cuts its way out of the shell with a sharp point on its bill. This point is known as an "egg tooth," and it will fall off soon after birth. (Many reptiles and birds have egg teeth, but they are unknown in other mammals.) By the time it is 4 months old, the baby platypus is about a foot long—half its adult size—and is learning how to swim and hunt.

Directions: Answer these questions about the duckbill platypus.

1. In what way is a duckbill platypus like other mammals? It gets milk from its mother.
2. In what way is it like a reptile? It hatches from a tough-skinned egg.
3. What other animal is in the class of mammal called "monotremes"? the spiny anteater
4. What makes up the diet of a platypus? earthworms, crayfish, tadpoles and insects
5. On what other animals would you see an "egg tooth"? many reptiles and birds

89

Recalling Details: Animals of Australia

Directions: Complete the chart with information from the selection on Australian animals.

	Gray Kangaroo	Koala	Wombat	Platypus
What are the animal's physical characteristics?	9 feet long 200 pounds marsupial good leaper fast mover	wooly round-eared marsupial good climber	marsupial walks on all fours strong claws and teeth up to 4 feet long 60 pounds	webbed feet duck-like bill fur, four legs hatches from egg poisonous spur 2 feet long good swimmer
What is the animal's habitat?	farmland of Australia	eucalyptus forests of eastern Australia	tunnels beneath cliffs and boulders	streams with muddy bottoms
What does the animal eat?	grasses, plants	eucalyptus leaves	grass, plants, roots	earthworms, crayfish, tadpoles, insects

90

Main Idea/Recalling Details: Land Down Under

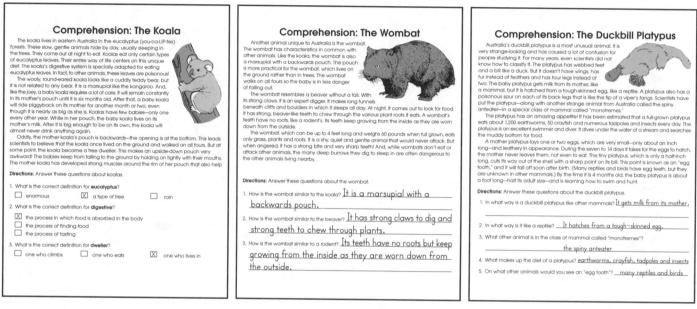

Australia and New Zealand are often referred to as the "land down under." The name, made popular by American soldiers stationed there during World War II, grew out of the idea that these two countries are opposite or below Europe on the globe. While Australia and New Zealand are often linked, they are individual countries, separated by more than 1,000 miles of ocean.

Their landscapes are quite different. New Zealand is made up of two main islands, North and South Island, which are nearly covered by snowy mountains. One of the most unusual and beautiful areas of New Zealand is the volcanic region around Lake Taupo on North Island. There you will see boiling springs, pools of steaming mud, hot-water geysers, small lakes with beds of brightly colored rocks and waterfalls. While most of the people of New Zealand live and work in the industrialized cities, dairy farming is most important to the country's economy. The New Zealanders eat more meat and butter than people anywhere else in the world, and they sell huge amounts to other countries.

As in Australia, many of the customs in New Zealand would be familiar to a traveler from America because the two countries were settled by British settlers hundreds of years ago. However, the native islanders have descended from Asian ancestors, so the remnants of ancient Eastern practices exist alongside the European way of life.

Directions: Answer these questions about New Zealand and Australia.

1. The main idea is:
   - ☐ Australia and New Zealand are often referred to as the "land down under."
   - ☒ While Australia and New Zealand are often linked, they are individual countries.
2. What is the correct definition for **landscape**?
   - ☒ natural scenery and features ☐ mountainsides ☐ natural resources
3. What is the correct definition for **economy**?
   - ☐ thrifty ☒ money management ☐ countryside
4. What is the nickname for Australia and New Zealand? land down under
5. What business is most important to the New Zealand economy? dairy farming

91

Writing: Australia

Directions: Write a three-paragraph informational essay on Australia. Discuss the land, its native people and its animals.

Answers will vary.

Writing Checklist

Reread your essay carefully.
- ☐ My essay makes sense.
- ☐ There are no jumps in ideas.
- ☐ I used correct punctuation.
- ☐ My essay is interesting.
- ☐ I have a good opening and ending.
- ☐ I used correct spelling.
- ☐ My essay is well-organized.

92

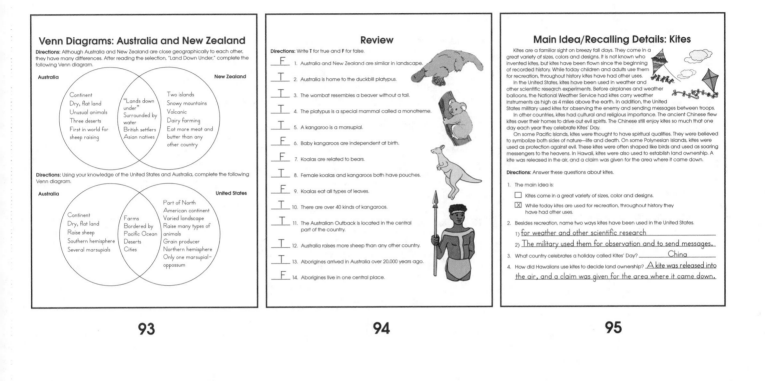

Venn Diagrams: Australia and New Zealand

Directions: Although Australia and New Zealand are close geographically to each other, they have many differences. After reading the selection, "Land Down Under," complete the following Venn diagram.

Australia | | New Zealand

Australia:
Continent
Dry, flat land
Unusual animals
Three deserts
First in world for sheep raising

Middle:
"Lands down under"
Surrounded by water
British settlers
Asian natives

New Zealand:
Two islands
Snowy mountains
Volcanic
Dairy farming
Eat more meat and butter than any other country

Directions: Using your knowledge of the United States and Australia, complete the following Venn diagram.

Australia | | United States

Australia:
Continent
Dry, flat land
Raise sheep
Southern hemisphere
Several marsupials

Middle:
Farms
Bordered by Pacific Ocean
Deserts
Cities

United States:
Part of North American continent
Varied landscape
Raise many types of animals
Grain producer
Northern hemisphere
Only one marsupial—oppossum

93

Review

Directions: Write **T** for true and **F** for false.

F 1. Australia and New Zealand are similar in landscape.

T 2. Australia is home to the duckbill platypus.

T 3. The wombat resembles a beaver without a tail.

T 4. The platypus is a special mammal called a monotreme.

T 5. A kangaroo is a marsupial.

F 6. Baby kangaroos are independent at birth.

F 7. Koalas are related to bears.

T 8. Female koalas and kangaroos both have pouches.

F 9. Koalas eat all types of leaves.

T 10. There are over 40 kinds of kangaroos.

T 11. The Australian Outback is located in the central part of the continent.

T 12. Australia raises more sheep than any other country.

T 13. Aborigines arrived in Australia over 20,000 years ago.

F 14. Aborigines live in one central place.

94

Main Idea/Recalling Details: Kites

Kites are a familiar sight on breezy fall days. They come in a great variety of sizes, colors and designs. It is not known who invented kites, but kites have been flown since the beginning of recorded history. While today children and adults use them for recreation, throughout history kites have had other uses.

In the United States, kites have been used in weather and other scientific research experiments. Before airplanes and weather balloons, the National Weather Service had kites carry weather instruments as high as 4 miles above the earth. In addition, the United States military used kites for observing the enemy and sending messages between troops.

In other countries, kites had cultural and religious importance. The ancient Chinese flew kites over their homes to drive out evil spirits. The Chinese still enjoy kites so much that one day each year they celebrate Kites' Day.

On some Pacific islands, kites were thought to have spiritual qualities. They were believed to symbolize both sides of nature—life and death. On some Polynesian islands, kites were used as protection against evil. These kites were often shaped like birds and used as soaring messengers to the heavens. In Hawaii, kites were also used to establish land ownership. A kite was released in the air, and a claim was given for the area where it came down.

Directions: Answer these questions about kites.

1. The main idea is:

☐ Kites come in a great variety of sizes, color and designs.

☒ While today children and adults are used for recreation, throughout history they have had other uses.

2. Besides recreation, name two ways kites have been used in the United States.

1) for weather and other scientific research

2) The military used them for observation and to send messages.

3. What country celebrates a holiday called Kites' Day? China

4. How did Hawaiians use kites to decide land ownership? A kite was released into the air, and a claim was given for the area where it came down.

95

Comprehension: Aerodynamics

Kites are able to fly because of the principle of aerodynamics. This big word simply means the study of forces that are put into action by moving air. Three main forces work to keep a heavier-than-air kite flying—lift, gravity and drag.

This is how it works: The flying lines, or strings, are attached to the kite to hold it at a slant. The wind pushes against the underside of the kite. At the same time, the wind rushes around the edges of the kite and "drags" some of the air from the upper side. This creates a partial vacuum there. The push of the air underneath it and the push of the air from the top, so the kite is held in the air. An airplane is held in the air in much the same way, except that it must keep moving rapidly to make the pressure above and below its wings different. The wind does this for the kite. In a steady airstream, a kite doesn't move backward or forward. It seems to be unaffected by gravity. This is possible because the lifting force of the wind overcomes the downward force of gravity.

If you have ever ridden a bicycle into a strong wind, you may have felt some of the forces of aerodynamics. If you held your hand out to your side, you could feel the air stream flowing around your hand. With your fingers pointed into the wind and your hand held level, there is little lift or drag. But if you raised your fingers slightly, the wind lifted your hand upwards. Raising your hand higher increases the drag and decreases the lift. Your hand is pushed downward. A kite flying in the sky is subject to these same forces.

Directions: Answer these questions about aerodynamics.

1. What is aerodynamics? the study of forces that are put into action by moving air

2. What three forces are at work to hold a kite in the air?

1) lift 2) gravity 3) drag

3. An airplane is held in the air in much the same way, except that it must keep moving rapidly to keep the air above and below its wings different.

(True) False

96

Comprehension: Getting Your Kite to Fly

There are some basic things to know about kite flying that can help you enjoy the sport more. Here are a few of the most important ones.

First, if you have ever seen someone flying a kite in a movie, you probably saw him or her get the kite off the ground by running into the wind. However, this is not the way to launch a kite. Most beginners will find a "high-start" launch to be the easiest. For a high-start launch, have a friend stand about 100 feet away, facing into the wind. Your friend should face you and hold the kite gently. Place some tension on the flying line by pulling gently on it. With a steady breeze behind you, tug gently on the line, and the kite will rise. If your kite begins to dive, don't panic or pull on the line. Dropping the reel will cause it to spin out of control and could cause someone to be hurt. Simply let the line go slack. This usually will right the kite in midair.

For a kite that is pulling hard away from you, have a friend stand behind you and take up the slack line as you bring it in. Hand over hand, pull down the kite. It is very important to have gloves on to do this, or you may burn or cut your hands. It is recommended that you always wear gloves while kite flying.

When two kite lines get crossed, pulling may cause enough friction to cut one or both of the lines. Instead of pulling, both fliers should walk toward one another until their lines uncross as they pass.

Directions: Circle **True** or **False** for these statements about kite flying.

1. To launch a kite, run into the wind holding the kite behind you. True (False)

2. In a high-start launch, a friend stands about 100 feet away from you, holding the kite. (True) False

3. If your kite begins to dive from the sky, immediately drop the reel. True (False)

4. It is recommended that you always wear gloves when kite flying. (True) False

97

Recalling Details: Kite Safety Rules

Because kite flying is a relaxed, easy-going sport, it is easy to have the mistaken belief that there are no dangers involved. However, like any sport, kite flying must be approached with care. Here are some important safety rules you should always follow while kite flying:

• Don't fly a kite in wet or stormy weather or use wet flying line.
• Don't fly a kite near electrical power lines, transmission towers or antennae. If your kite does get caught in one of these, walk away and leave it! If you must get the kite back, contact your local electric company.
• Don't use wire for flying line.
• Don't use metal for any part of the kite.
• Don't fly a kite near a street or in crowded areas.
• Don't fly a kite in a field or other area that has rocks or other objects you could trip over.
• Don't walk backwards without looking behind you.
• Don't fly a kite around trees. (If your kite does happen to get caught in a tree, let the line go slack. Sometimes the wind can work it free.)
• Don't fly a kite using unfamiliar equipment. A reel spinning out of control can be quite dangerous.
• Don't fly a kite near an airport.
• Don't fly a very large kite without proper guidance.
• Do wear protective gloves to avoid burns on your hands from rapidly unwinding line.
• Do use flying line that has been tested for the type and size of kite you are using.

Directions: Answer these questions about kite safety. Answers may include:

1. List three things you should never fly a kite around.

1) trees 2) airport 3) electrical power lines

2. What should you do if your kite gets caught in a tree? Let the line go slack, and the wind may work it free.

3. What material should you never use in any part of your kite? metal

98

Recalling Details: Aviation Pioneer

Lawrence Hargrave was born in Middlesex, England, in 1850. When he was a teenager, his family moved to Australia. There Hargrave went to work for the Australian Stream and Navigation Company, where he spent 5 years gaining practical experience in engineering. He soon became interested in artificial flight.

Hargrave wanted to develop a stable lifting surface that could be used for flying. This goal led to his invention of the box kite, one of the seven basic models. In 1894, he carried out kite experiments along the beaches near his home. One day, in front of onlookers, he was lifted above the beach and out over the sea by four of his box kites. These experiments were very important to the development of air travel, although Hargrave has received little credit for it. In fact, because of his modesty, Hargrave failed to get a patent on his box kite. He spent more than 30 years studying flying, offering many inventions, including a rotary engine.

In 1906, Hargrave began looking for a home for his collection of nearly 200 models of kites and flying machines. After being rejected by several governments, his collection was accepted at a technological museum in Munich, Germany. Unfortunately, many of these models were destroyed during World War I.

Directions: Answer these questions about Lawrence Hargrave.

1. For what kite design was Lawrence Hargrave known? _box kite_

2. What was Hargrave trying to create when he made this kite?
a stable lifting surface that could be used for flying

3. What was one of the inventions Hargrave contributed to aviation? _____
the rotary engine

4. Where was Hargrave's collection of kites and flying machines finally housed?
a technological museum in Munich, Germany

99

Main Idea/Recalling Details: A Kite in History

In June 1752, Benjamin Franklin proved that lightning was a type of electricity by flying a kite with a key tied to the bottom of the line during a thunderstorm. Before his experiment, many people thought that lightning was a supernatural power.

After the success of his experiment, Franklin figured that if lightning could be drawn to a kite in a storm, it could be safely redirected into the ground by a metal rod attached to a house. His idea was met with much doubt, but lightning rods were soon seen on buildings in many of the colonies and later in Europe. During the years between 1683 and 1789, studying the universe and laws of nature was of tremendous importance. It was during this Age of Reason, as it was known, that Franklin's kite experiment gained him international fame and respect. He was elected to the Royal Society of London and the French Academy of Sciences, among other honors.

More than 20 years after his bold experiment, American patriots were enduring many hardships in their struggles for freedom from England. The colonial troops had shortages of guns, gun powder and food. France was sending supplies but not as much as was needed. Benjamin Franklin was chosen to go to France to persuade the French to aid the American cause. Franklin's reputation as a brilliant scientist earned him a hero's welcome there. The French people were so impressed by him that they wanted to help the colonies, even during a time when they could barely afford it. The supplies sent by the French were instrumental to the colonists in winning the war. And it all started with a kite.

Directions: Answer these questions about Ben Franklin and his historical kite.

1. The main idea is:

[X] A kite played a role in the American Revolution and gained a spot in history books.

[ ] Benjamin Franklin proved that lightning was a type of electricity by flying a kite with a key tied to the bottom of the line during a storm.

2. From his kite and key experiment, what did Franklin invent? _lightning rod_

3. What was the era between 1683 and 1789 known as? _Age of Reason_

4. Why was Franklin sent to France in 1776? _to persuade the French to aid the American struggle for freedom from England_

100

Summarizing: Pioneers

Directions: Think about the lives and accomplishments of Ben Franklin and Lawrence Hargrave. Write one paragraph about each, summarizing what you have learned about these two men.

| Answers should include: | Ben Franklin |

1752 kite-and-key experiment
studied universe and laws of nature
ambassador to France
born in Boston in 1706
apprentice printer

| Answers should include: | Lawrence Hargrave |

born in Middlesex, England, in 1850
engineer
invented box kite
used four box kites to lift himself
studied flying for 30 years, creating many inventions

Writing Checklist

Reread your paragraphs carefully.

[ ] My paragraphs make sense.   [ ] I used correct spelling.
[ ] I used correct punctuation.   [ ] My paragraphs are well-organized.
[ ] I have a good opening and ending.   [ ] My paragraphs are interesting.

101

Review

Directions: Number in order the steps for how to launch a kite.

_5_ With a steady breeze behind you, gently pull on the line.
_3_ Have your friend face you and gently hold the kite.
_6_ Your kite will rise.
_2_ Have your friend face into the wind.
_4_ Place some tension on the flying line by pulling on it.
_1_ Have a friend stand about 100 feet away from you.

Directions: Write **True** or **False** for these statements about kite safety.

True 1. You should not use wire for flying line.
False 2. Fly any size kite you wish as long as you have the right flying line.
True 3. If your kite gets caught in a tree, let the line go slack.
False 4. It's okay to fly a kite in the rain.
True 5. You should not fly a kite in crowded areas.
False 6. You can use metal on your kite as long as it's not the flying line itself.
False 7. You don't need to wear gloves unless you're flying a very large kite.
True 8. You should not fly a kite around an airport.
False 9. If your kite gets caught in power lines, just tug the line gently until it works free.
False 10. The best place to fly a kite is in a large field.

102

Review

Directions: Answer these questions about kites.

Sample answers:

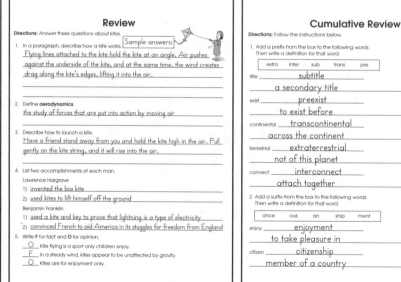

1. In a paragraph, describe how a kite works.
Flying lines attached to the kite hold the kite at an angle. Air pushes against the underside of the kite, and at the same time, the wind creates drag along the kite's edges, lifting it into the air.

2. Define **aerodynamics**.
the study of forces that are put into action by moving air

3. Describe how to launch a kite.
Have a friend stand away from you and hold the kite high in the air. Pull gently on the kite string, and it will rise into the air.

4. List two accomplishments of each man.
Lawrence Hargrave
1) _invented the box kite_
2) _used kites to lift himself off the ground_
Benjamin Franklin
1) _used a kite and key to prove that lightning is a type of electricity_
2) _convinced French to aid America in its struggles for freedom from England_

5. Write **F** for fact and **O** for opinion.
_O_ Kite flying is a sport only children enjoy.
_F_ In a steady wind, kites appear to be unaffected by gravity.
_O_ Kites are for enjoyment only.

103

Cumulative Review

Directions: Follow the instructions below.

1. Add a prefix from the box to the following words. Then write a definition for that word.

| extra | inter | sub | trans | pre |

title _subtitle_
a secondary title

exist _preexist_
to exist before

continental _transcontinental_
across the continent

terrestrial _extraterrestrial_
not of this planet

connect _interconnect_
attach together

2. Add a suffix from the box to the following words. Then write a definition for that word.

| ance | ous | an | ship | ment |

enjoy _enjoyment_
to take pleasure in

citizen _citizenship_
member of a country

104

Cumulative Review

Africa __African__
__of or from Africa__

mischief __mischievous__
__full of mischief__

perform __performance__
__a show__

3. Write the correct definition for the bold homograph.

Use a **minute** amount of detergent in that machine.
__very small portion__

I'll have to **resort** to using my allowance to make the purchase.
__go back to the last option__

Contracts are used in most business agreements.
__legal documents__

4. Write **M** if the sentence contains a metaphor. Write **S** if it contains a simile.

__S__ Waves hit the beach like a thousand hammers.
__S__ He runs like the wind.
__M__ I am a turtle when it comes to finishing a project.
__S__ She was as quiet as a mouse creeping up behind him.
__M__ The young child's hair was spun gold in the sunlight.

5. The following sentence demonstrates what figure of speech? __idiom__

The fight they had was soon water under the bridge.

6. A word's __denotation__ is its exact meaning.

A word's __connotation__ is the idea associated with the word.

105

Cumulative Review

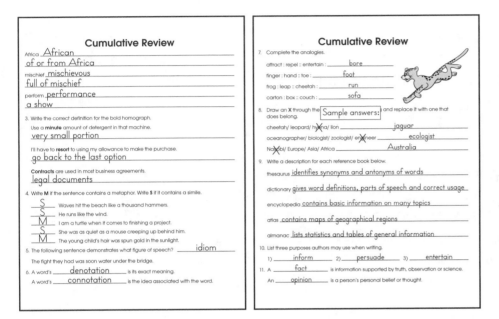

7. Complete the analogies.

attract : repel :: entertain : __bore__

finger : hand :: toe : __foot__

frog : leap :: cheetah : __run__

carton : box :: couch : __sofa__

8. Draw an **X** through the [Sample answers:] and replace it with one that does belong.

cheetah/ leopard/ hy~~e~~na/ lion __jaguar__

oceanographer/ biologist/ zoologist/ en~~g~~ineer __ecologist__

Na~~i~~robi/ Europe/ Asia/ Africa __Australia__

9. Write a description for each reference book below.

thesaurus __identifies synonyms and antonyms of words__

dictionary __gives word definitions, parts of speech and correct usage__

encyclopedia __contains basic information on many topics__

atlas __contains maps of geographical regions__

almanac __lists statistics and tables of general information__

10. List three purposes authors may use when writing.

1) __inform__   2) __persuade__   3) __entertain__

11. A __fact__ is information supported by truth, observation or science.

An __opinion__ is a person's personal belief or thought.

106

Teaching Suggestions

Cause and Effect

Invite your child to read the newspaper front page, circling the causes of an event and underlining the effects.

Have your child write cause-and-effect statements for his/her daily activities. For example: I hit the snooze button on my alarm clock, so I was late for school. I practiced fielding ground balls over the weekend, so I did much better at baseball practice.

Classifying

Give your child several category names, and invite him/her to provide several examples. For example: Modes of Transportation—car, train, bicycle, airplane, wheelchair, horse and buggy. See how many examples you can come up with for each category. Then provide your child with several examples and ask him/her to name the category. For example: sugar, candy, honey, fruit—Sweet Things.

Comprehension

When you read to or with your child, discuss details of the story. Ask your child about the sequence of events—beginning, middle and end.

Ask your child questions about the story before you begin reading. For example: What do you think the illustration on the book cover means? Will this be an adventure story? A fantasy story? A true story? What do you think the title means? What do you think will happen to (character's name)?

Reading Extensions

Colonial America
Have your child research famous Colonial women such as Betsy Ross, Pocahontas and Sacajawea. Write an informational paragraph about each woman's accomplishments. Invite your child to read more about the Puritans and the Quakers, then complete a Venn diagram comparing the two groups.

Have your child make a time line of important Colonial America events. He/she can include events such as the arrival at Plymouth Rock, the first Thanksgiving, the Revolutionary War and the signing of the Declaration of Independence.

Teaching Suggestions

Weather
Collect the daily newspaper weather map for one week. Have your child go on a scavenger hunt for weather information such as:
> Yesterday's High
> Tomorrow's Forecast
> Temperature in Paris, France
> Pollen Count
> Pollution Index

Give your child weather math problems to solve such as:
> Compute the average daily temperature forecast for 1 week.
> Change the high and low temperatures for the week from Fahrenheit to Celsius.

Invite your child to research earthquakes and compare it to weather phenomena such as tornadoes, hurricanes and thunderstorms. Which is a most devastating force of nature? Compare damage in money and casualties for each for a 10-year period in the United States. Ask your child to record his/her findings.

Australia
Ask your child to find a picture of the Australian flag and compare it to the United States flag. How are the flags alike? Different? What symbols are on the flags, and what do they represent? Invite your child to write a brief paragraph comparing and contrasting the two flags.

Have your child research the number of sheep in Australia vs. the number of people. Have him/her create bar and circle graphs showing this information.

Invite your child to do additional research on the Aborigine culture. What dangers do they face in the future? What is their diet? What traditions do they have?

Have your child create a habitat display on an Australian animal. Divide a poster board into four equal sections. In the top left section, have him/her write an informational report about the animal. In the top right, have him/her make a web of animals to whom it is related. In the bottom left, have your child write a poem about the animal. Finally, in the last section, your child can draw the animal.

Teaching Suggestions

Kites

Invite your child to read more about Benjamin Franklin's kite and key experiment; then write a one-paragraph informational essay about what was discovered. How was this discovery later applied in the world of science?

Have your child go to the library and check out a book illustrating different types of kites, including box kites, stunt kites, flat kites and sled kites. Have your child describe what makes the kites alike and what makes them different?

Many kite terms are also weather terms. Encourage your child to find the definitions for the following words: **drag**, **lift**, **turbulence**, **upwind**, **wind speed** and **downwind**. Ask your child to explain how these terms apply to kite flying. Or better yet, take your child out to fly a kite, and ask him/her to use these terms in the process!

Vocabulary Building

Have your child learn a new word each week. You may select a word from your child's school subjects such as math, reading, spelling, and so on. Encourage him/her to use the word as much as possible during that week. Also encourage family members to use the word for reinforcement.

Have your child think of synonyms for words he/she may "overuse." For example: **Cold** can be converted to **frosty**, **icy**, **freezing**, **chilly**, **cool**, and so on.

Writing

Read the editorial section of your local newspaper with your child. This section includes opinion essays. Invite your child to write a sample "Letter to the Editor" describing something he/she feels strongly about. If it is currently relevant in your community, help him/her send it to the paper.

Have your child keep a daily journal during a vacation. He/she can record sights, sounds and smells; favorite destinations; and so on. Collect and read brochures about various places and activities. At the end of the vacation, have your child reread his/her journal and write a short essay about vacation highlights.